HOW **NOT** TO MOVE BACK IN WITH YOUR PARENTS

THE YOUNG PERSON'S GUIDE TO FINANCIAL EMPOWERMENT

ROB CARRICK

 DOUBLEDAY CANADA

Doubleday Canada and colophon are registered trademarks

Library and Archives Canada Cataloguing in Publication

Carrick, Rob, 1962-
    How not to move back in with your parents: the young person's complete guide to financial empowerment / Rob Carrick.

ISBN 978-0-385-67192-7

    1. Youth--Canada--Finance, Personal--Juvenile literature.
2. Teenagers--Canada--Finance, Personal--Juvenile literature.
3. Finance, Personal--Canada--Juvenile literature. I. Title.

HG179.C375 2012   j332.024'008350971   C2011-907435-4

Cover and text design: Paul Dotey
Printed and bound in the USA

Published in Canada by Doubleday Canada,
a division of Random House of Canada Limited

www.randomhouse.ca

10 9 8 7 6 5 4 3 2 1

CONTENTS

INTRODUCTION   1

ONE: AFFORDING COLLEGE OR UNIVERSITY   7
- The Big Picture on Where the Money Will Come From
- Why RESPs Rule
- For RESP Procrastinators
- RESP Investing Basics
- Putting RESPs to Use
- Artists, Athletes and Other Non-Academic Types
- Finding Financial Help Through Scholarships
- Thinking Ahead to University
- Consider the Gap Year
- Thoughts on What to Study
- What It *Really* Costs to Attend College or University
- The Student's Dilemma: Should You Stay or Should You Go?
- Student Borrowing Basics
- Hotlist: Tips for Saving Money in Your Student Years
- It's Payback Time
- How Paying Back Student Debt Works
- A Student's Guide to Interest Rates and Borrowing Costs
- Sorry to Nag, But . . .

- The Debt Trap: How Parents Can Help
- Tax Tips for Students
- Online Tools for Students
- **CASE STUDY: Stephen**

TWO: HOW TO HANDLE DEBT, BOTH IN SCHOOL   **41**
AND AFTERWARD
- Where Bad Attitudes About Credit Begin
- Ways Parents Can Raise Financially Smart Kids
- The Scandal of Student Credit Cards
- Student Credit Card Rundown
- Credit Cards: One Family's Story
- Should Your Parents Give You a Credit Card
  for Emergencies?
- How to Build a Good Credit Rating
- Hotlist: Expert Tips on Building a Solid Credit
  Rating
- Into the Workforce
- Should You Ask Your Parents to Co-Sign a Loan?
- Loan Basics
- Debt as a Way of Life
- **CASE STUDY: Jamie**

THREE: YOU AND YOUR BANK   **64**
- Recognize Your Potential
- Meet the Banks
- Student Banking
- The Wonders of No-Fee Chequing Accounts
- Pass This On to Younger Siblings

- Post-Graduation Banking Needs, Part One
- Post-Graduation Banking Needs, Part Two
- The End of Cheques?
- Hotlist: Top Banking Blunders to Avoid

FOUR: SAVING, BUDGETING AND WHAT TO DO IF YOU HAVE TO MOVE BACK HOME   80
- Post-Graduation Financial Priorities
- An Introduction to Budgeting
- Budgeting Basics
- A Sample Budget
- Let Technology Do Your Budgeting for You
- Credit vs. Debit vs. Cash for Day-to-Day Spending
- Hotlist: Five Rookie Financial Mistakes to Avoid
- When Plans Go Awry: Introducing the Boomerang Generation
- I Belong to the Boomerang Generation (And I Can Take It or Leave It Each Time)
- Hotlist: How to Handle the 'Rents If You Have to Move Back Home
- Tougher Economic Times?
- **CASE STUDY: Sarah**

FIVE: LOOKING TO THE FUTURE: RRSPs AND TFSAs   99
- What Your Parents Can Contribute
- Order of Operations: What to Do First
- RRSPs for Twentysomethings: One Expert's Perspective

- The ABCs of RRSPs
- Parental Guidance on RRSPs
- Investing in RRSPs 101
- What About Your Parents' Retirement Savings?
- Three Paths for Starting an RRSP
- The Smartest RRSP Strategy of Them All
- Leaky RRSPs
- Tax-Free Savings Accounts vs. RRSPs for Retirement Savings
- RRSPs & TFSAs: A Tax Expert's View
- TFSAs as Gifts
- A Few Final Points in Favour of RRSPs
- An Introduction to Pension Plans for Those Lucky Enough to Find Jobs Offering Them
- Hotlist: Ten Things You Need to Know About Your Company Pension Plan

SIX: MOBILITY: OR, CARS AND YOU 134

- Rethinking the Car
- Introducing the Car-Sharing Service
- Bikes Are Great, Too
- Okay, You Still Want a Car
- Can Your Parents Help You Drive a Hard Bargain?
- Get Your Grad Discount
- Buying vs. Leasing
- The Last Word on Cars
- **CASE STUDY: Laura**

SEVEN: BUYING A HOME   **146**

- Our Housing Obsession
- Hotlist: Three Money Myths About Houses
- The R-Word (Renting)
- More Thoughts on Renting
- How to Save for a Home
- The First-Time Homebuyers' Tax Credit
- Getting Help from the 'Rents to Buy a House
- Can You Afford a House?
- Everyday Home Economics
- Hotlist: Seven Killer Costs of Home Ownership That Will Surprise First-Time Buyers
- How to Tell When You're Ready to Buy
- Hotlist: Top Mortgage Tips for First-Time Homebuyers
- Arranging Your First Mortgage
- The Great Debate: Variable or Fixed Rate
- Other Mortgage Details
- Moving In
- **CASE STUDY: Nathan**

EIGHT: WEDDINGS AND KIDS   **182**

- Weddings: You, Your Parents and the High Cost of Getting Married
- When Your Parents Should Think Twice About Helping You Financially for Weddings or Anything Else
- Money Talk, Pre-Marriage
- Tips for Saving Money on a Wedding

- Money Talk for Newlyweds or Those Who Live Together
- Financial Equality Issues Among the Newly Married
- Baby Talk
- Maternity and Parental Benefits: Your Salary as the Stay-at-Home Parent of an Infant
- Hotlist: Top Five Financial Mistakes New Parents Make
- Back to Work: Or, Welcome to Daycare
- Tax Tips for Parents
- What About the Grandparents?
- **CASE STUDY: Meghan**

NINE: INSURANCE AND WILLS   **204**
- Renters Insurance, a.k.a. Tenants Insurance
- Home and Auto Insurance
- Home Insurance Basics
- Car Insurance
- Life Insurance
- Hotlist: Top Reasons Not to Buy Mortgage Life Insurance from Your Bank
- How Term Life Quotes Stack Up
- Wills

CONCLUSION   **218**
INDEX   **223**

INTRODUCTION

The young people of today? I feel for you because you've got money problems. The cost of attending university or college is rising fast, and only students seem to care much. The job market is tougher than ever, houses are expensive and gas prices are on a one-way trip to exorbitant. Borrowing money is the easy solution to these problems, and God knows the older generation has embraced debt.

But times are different now. Following the Great Recession, which ended the last decade, the standards for responsible adult financial behaviour are higher. In government and in public schools, financial literacy is a big theme. Saving is in and unrestrained consumption is out. It's confusing as hell out there in the world now if you're in your twenties or thirties. On one hand, our consumer culture is telling you to live it up, and on the other, you're being told to spend and save wisely so you don't end up with the sort of financial problems that may burden your parents.

The pressure is on, but help is at hand. Whether you're in your late teens, your twenties or your thirties, this book is your personal finance manual. We'll start with the financial ins and outs of attending college or university and then work our way forward through the milestones of a first credit card and first car, starting an RRSP and a TFSA, buying a home and then starting a family. Securing your financial independence is the main goal here, but we'll also look at times when the smart move is to ask for advice or assistance from your parents.

The family approach is how we do things now that the School of Hard Knocks (Financial Division) is closed down. You can't learn from your mistakes the way your parents and grandparents may have done. The world of money is just too dangerous these days. That's the lesson of the financial shocks of the past several years. In fact, a very good case can be made that a lot of this turmoil was a result of people making avoidable mistakes with their finances.

What happens to twenty- and thirtysomethings who don't find their way in the world of money? In the long term, mistakes made with debt can cost them the opportunity to afford the home they've always wanted, the trips they planned and a comfortable retirement. In the short term, they may be forced to join what's being called the Boomerang Generation. That's the term used to describe people who left home to go to university and were then forced by financial problems to move back home.

Let's be honest here: part of the problem with people graduating from university and establishing themselves in the workforce is that they aren't helping themselves as much as they could be. A financial adviser I know of named Kurt Rosentreter zeroed in on this subject in a blistering commentary in which he describes the massive hole he sees young adults digging themselves into these days (the title: "Canadian 30-Year-Olds Are Screwed"). He worries these young adults are putting more time into Internet surfing than managing their money. He worries they think too much about what they want to buy and not enough about the discipline of saving. He worries they're spending too much on houses without thinking about the impact on their ability to afford everything else in life. And he worries they're moving from employer to employer without pension plans or any retirement savings of their own.

Rosentreter argues that mistakes made by today's young adults will come together when they reach about age 50 to create a financial nightmare. They'll be close to retirement, their children will be ready to go to college or university and they will have made almost no serious headway in savings. If they don't win the lottery, they'll have to work into their seventies.

Yes, this is a pessimistic and perhaps alarmist view. But it's also a realistic assessment of what's ahead for young adults who don't understand that the financial decisions they make in the decade or two after high school will very likely shape the rest of their lives.

I'm 48 as I write this, but I remember both the good and the bad financial decisions I made decades back. You'll read about them here, and you'll also get the benefit of my more than a decade spent as personal-finance columnist for *The Globe and Mail*. I know the money challenges people face today. I've heard the success stories and the disasters.

You'll find no lectures here, just clear and unbiased guidance on how you can get the best possible financial start to life as an adult. Let's get to work.

YOU AND YOUR PARENTS: DIFFERENT PERSPECTIVES ON FINANCIAL MATTERS

To get some ideas on how different generations view matters like debt and spending, I consulted Laura Parsons, a mortgage expert at Bank of Montreal with more than twenty-five years of experience in the financial industry. Here are some of her thoughts:

- **Family dynamics.** People are getting married later and starting families later; also, dual-income families are much more common than they used to be.
- **Style of banking.** Your generation does everything electronically (online, ATM and phone), whereas those in the previous generation were much more willing to do their banking in actual banks; interestingly, Parsons predicts an upswing in branch banking as people seek the personal touch in an impersonal online world.
- **Spending.** Young adults today put more emphasis on having fun and buying all the latest toys (partly because

they're starting families later). Also, they're very open to debt in forms like car loans, mortgages and even don't-pay-a-cent events.

- **Day-to-day finances.** Balancing chequebooks is passé; today's young people are more likely to use credit cards and therefore less likely to track their regular spending through the week.
- **Houses.** Parents were more willing to move into a modest home and either fix it up or move up later on; today's young people want it all right away—they're willing to renovate and they're right on top of deluxe details like granite countertops.

ONE

AFFORDING COLLEGE OR UNIVERSITY

Whatever the cost of getting a quality post-secondary education, it's worth it. That's a bold statement, given that tuition fees at universities and colleges are soaring in a way that staggers even a hardened financial observer like me. But let's be realistic. In today's hypercompetitive world, most young people need more than a high school education to gain the skills and knowledge necessary to build a career that's both emotionally and financially rewarding.

But the cost! When I attended university as an undergraduate in the early 1980s, I recall paying roughly $1,000 per year in tuition. The most recent Statistics Canada estimate of average annual university tuition as this book was being written: $5,138. That works out to an annual average increase of about 5.6 per cent since my student days, which compares to an average annual inflation rate of 2.6 per cent over the same time frame. The exact numbers here don't matter as much as the fact that the cost of attending university has been rising at a much faster rate than the cost of almost everything else. Forget about governments doing much to alleviate this trend; they're either too indebted or too unmotivated to make it more affordable for students to attend college or university.

Note that we're talking here about tuition costs alone. Books and supplies could easily add another $1,500 in annual costs. And then there are living expenses if you go away to school. Figure on paying roughly $15,000 to $20,000 in total per year to attend university out of town.

I've come across a few different attitudes toward the cost of a post-secondary education. Some parents are saving diligently in registered education savings plans (RESPs) in order to at least reduce the amount their kids will need to borrow. Others believe that students have to take financial responsibility for their own lives, and that they might as well start with the cost of college or university. When I was a student, that approach was feasible. Today, it's not. If the burden of paying for a university or college education is left strictly on students, we risk creating a generation of adults stuck in a twilight zone of debt that for too long holds them back from becoming full participants in the economy. There are all kinds of worrying implications here. Think about the housing market—who's going to buy all the houses that aging baby boomers are selling if young adults can't afford to get into the market until age 35? And how are these 35-year-olds going to save for retirement if they trade their student debt for twenty-five or thirty years of mortgage debt?

You and your parents have to work together to pay for a post-secondary education. Plan carefully, because the moves you make before you start college or university will have a big effect on what comes next in your financial life.

THE BIG PICTURE ON WHERE THE MONEY WILL COME FROM

There are four key sources of money to help students pay for tuition and other expenses associated with going to university or college. One is the registered education savings plan, which parents, ideally, set up for their children as early as possible and to which regular contributions are made over the years. Another is the student's own savings, which would consist of money set aside from gifts and such over the years, as well as income from part-time jobs. A third source of money is scholarships—more on those shortly—and the fourth is the dreaded, but often indispensable, student loan.

The most recent statistics available show that close to 60 per cent of students in college or university graduate with debt, which tells us that student loans are a fact of life in today's world. Don't misunderstand. Student loans are not becoming more manageable or comfortable as they become ubiquitous. Quite the opposite, in fact. A Statistics Canada study carried out in 1995 showed that fewer than half of grads went into debt of any kind (government, bank, loans from family) to pay for college or university. The average amount borrowed has increased, too. StatsCan's data shows the average debt load for grads who borrowed was $15,200 back in 1995. The Canadian Alliance of Student Associations says a comparable recent number would be $26,680.

In the United States, the term "anti-dowry" was recently coined to describe young adults who bring large student debts to their marriage and thereby delay home-buying and other milestones. Tuitions aren't as expensive here, so the student debt issue hasn't received as much attention. But it's out there and it's getting worse. Students, don't take any guff from adults who tell you they had student loans back in the day and they made out fine. It *is* different today.

Let's start to get a handle on student debt. The goal with student loans should be to borrow as little as possible to top up other sources of money that will be used to cover tuition and other costs. Every dollar students borrow today becomes a dollar they have to pay back later, plus interest. If you're a student who has never held a job and never had to manage debts and other obligations, this probably won't impress you much. Trust me, though: when you've graduated from university and landed a job with decent pay, you'll be thinking about spending money on yourself. Furnishing your apartment, buying a car, taking trips, enjoying life. You will *not* want to shovel large chunks of money into repaying your student loans. And yet, that's exactly the position you'll be in if you take out student loans. Keep those loans as small as possible and you reach financial freedom sooner.

FACTS AND FIGURES ON STUDENT DEBT

As this data from the Canadian Alliance of Student Associations shows, debt is hard to avoid when you're a student attending college or university. So learn to handle it properly.

Average undergrad tuition in 2010–11	$5,138
Recent trend for tuition increases	+17% over past four years
Percentage of students graduating with debt	58%
Average cumulative debt level	$26,680 per person
Student loan default rate	16%
Default trend in 2004	28%

Notes: Statistics Canada figures show somewhat lower debt levels, but they reflect only borrowing through government programs and not through banks as well. The Canadian Federation of Students website has an online student debt clock that tallies money owing on student loans. Check the latest number here: http://www.cfs-fcee.ca/html/english/home/index.php.

WHY RESPs RULE

If your parents have any desire to help you afford a post-secondary education, this is how they should be going about it. Ideally, they will have set up a registered education savings plan when you were born and then contributed gradually over the years. My wife and I have for years made automatic monthly contributions into a self-directed RESP we set up for our two sons through an online brokerage. As soon as you have kids, you should start your own RESP investment plan.

There are two excellent reasons to make use of RESPs. One is the Canada Education Savings Grant (CESG), through which the federal government will add twenty cents to each dollar contributed to an RESP, up to a total of $500 annually per beneficiary and a lifetime maximum of $7,200. The second argument in favour of RESPs is that they allow savings to compound tax-free. RESP withdrawals will in some cases be considered taxable income in the hands of a beneficiary, but don't worry too much about that. As you'll read later on in this chapter, students often don't end up having to pay income taxes. Note: There is no tax deduction for a contribution to an RESP, as there is with a registered retirement savings plan.

RESPs have been around since 1974, but they became popular only when the CESG was introduced in 1998. Actually, popular isn't really the word, because my sense is that RESPs are underutilized to the point of negligence on the part of some parents. I know well how many demands there are on a family's money—daily expenses, maintaining an emergency fund, contributing to retirement savings and then putting money into registered retirement savings plans, tax-free savings accounts (TFSAs) and RESPs. Choices have to be made, and too often RESPs aren't getting chosen. When you compare the uptake of the RESP against the fairly new TFSA, you have to wonder if there are some parents who have their financial priorities out of whack.

In mid-2010, eighteen months after they were introduced, TFSAs had captured $29.8 billion in assets. The comparable amount in RESPs at June 20, 2010, was $26.6 billion. TFSAs are a savings vehicle with universal appeal, while RESPs are a niche product. But the speed with which TFSA assets shot ahead of RESPs suggests that the registered education savings plan isn't getting used enough. This view is bolstered by the results of polling conducted by Studentawards.com, an online directory of scholarships available to students. Studentawards found that only 37 per cent of high school students had an RESP waiting for them, and the vast majority had less than $5,000 sitting in a plan. The Canadian Alliance of Student Associations has produced even more dismal numbers. They suggest only about 14 per cent of post-secondary students are using RESPs to help pay their educational costs. These numbers on RESP usage are pitiful and may even border on parental neglect in some cases.

RESPs can be set up by relatives or non-relatives. So if your folks are having trouble finding enough cash to contribute to a plan, maybe your grandparents can help out. Same for aunts, uncles and any other well-meaning relatives. Note that there are two kinds of RESPs. One is the individual plan, which is set up for one beneficiary and can be opened by anyone, blood relative or not. The other is a family plan, which can have multiple beneficiaries and must be opened by a parent, grandparent or sibling (related by blood or adoption).

One more point regarding RESPs is that they're not just for mainstream colleges and universities. Trade schools, covering everything from hair and aesthetics to culinary arts, massage and audio-visual arts, are included, and so are many foreign educational institutions.

A quick word about RESP contribution limits, just to give you an idea of how much potential money can go into these savings vehicles: the lifetime cap per beneficiary is $50,000.

FOR RESP PROCRASTINATORS

An RESP (specifically, an individual plan) can be set up on your behalf at any time, no matter your age, but you can receive the Canada Education Savings Grant only if you are 17 or younger.

There are some conditions that apply to your eligibility to receive grant money when you're 16 and 17—the years just before university, in other words. First, $2,000 must have been contributed to your plan before the year you turned 16, and not withdrawn. Alternatively, you can be eligible for grant money if $100 was contributed to your plan in any four years before the year you turned 16.

Let's say your parents started and funded your RESP just in time for you to collect the Canada Education Savings Grant. In the years you were 15, 16 and 17, they could contribute $5,000 per year and collect $1,000 annually in CESG. There's a $500 limit on CESG payable for the current year, plus you can get an additional maximum of $500 for a previous year in which you could have received the grant but did not. The total grant money available for any one year is $1,000.

RESP INVESTING BASICS

Managing an RESP is like a dress rehearsal for handling a registered retirement savings plan (RRSP), which you'll read all about in Chapter Five. For both kinds of plan, a time will come when the priority changes from trying to build up your savings to protecting what you've already earned.

In the years when you were growing from a baby to a toddler to a primary school student, your parents could afford to take a reasonably aggressive investing stance by putting roughly half to two-thirds of your RESP in the stock markets. Then, as the years went by, they should have ratcheted down the stock market exposure in the plan every few years. As you begin university or college, the mix in your RESP should be something along the lines of 25 per cent stocks at most and the rest in comparatively safe stuff like GICs. There's even an argument for staying out of the stock market entirely once you start drawing income from an RESP.

Another rule is to keep one or two years' worth of educational expenses in cash—money market funds, high-interest savings accounts or Treasury bills. The benefit: no matter what the stock markets are doing when it comes time to cash in some RESP money to pay your bills, you'll have ready cash.

RESP INVESTING TIP

When buying GICs or bonds, arrange for them to mature in July so as to have cash ready and waiting to pay tuition and other costs that will mount in the lead-up to September. Universities are like businesses—they expect customers to pay on time.

PUTTING RESPs TO USE

First off, let's be clear about who controls RESPs—it's your parents, technically known as subscribers. Students, as beneficiaries, do not get to make their own RESP withdrawals as needed. That said, you and your parents will want to work together to make use of the money in the plan. Some advance planning is called for here. Start simply by calculating your annual post-secondary educational costs—we'll look at this in more detail later in this chapter—and then multiplying by the number of years your program requires. It's smart to factor in an inflation rate of 3 to 5 per cent for post-secondary costs each year. Another suggestion I've heard is to take your estimated cost of education and then add an additional 20 to 30 per cent to cover potential cost increases ahead.

The documentation your parents need to make a withdrawal from an RESP is proof of your enrolment in an approved post-secondary institution (a letter of enrolment, invoice for tuition fees) and a completed RESP withdrawal form. Once the money is withdrawn, it can be used to cover tuition, books, living expenses or anything else. After the withdrawal, there's no oversight of what RESP money is spent on.

Now comes the complex part of RESP withdrawals from your parents' point of view. Although they might see the money sitting your RESP as a lump sum of savings, it's actually divided into two categories. One represents the contributions they made to the plan over the years, while the other is the accumulated income. This latter category is made up of grant money received from the federal government, as well as interest, dividends and capital gains from the money invested in the RESP.

The distinction between accumulated income and your contribution amount is important because it's connected to the two types of withdrawals parents can make from an RESP. One is what's known as a Post-Secondary Education (PSE) payment—that's money withdrawn from the contribution portion of the RESP, or in other words, your parents' own money. The other withdrawal is called an Education Assistance Payment (EAP)—that's from the accumulated income.

There are a couple of considerations in deciding whether you and your parents want to make a withdrawal as a PSE payment or an EAP. One is tax-related. Money taken out through a PSE payment is non-taxable—remember, this is money your parents put into the plan. EAPs are considered taxable income for the student who receives them. If you have a higher-than-normal income one year because of a good summer job, it might make sense to use a PSE payment instead of an EAP.

Another consideration is that your parents can't request an EAP of more than $5,000 in the first thirteen weeks you attend college or university. They can top this up with money taken from their RESP contributions (that would be a PSE withdrawal), but they should think twice about that early on because students sometimes drop out quickly in their first year, or their circumstances can change.

If your parents check the account statements for your RESP, it's unlikely they will find a running tally of their contributions, grant money received and investment gains. So when it comes time to make a withdrawal, they should contact the investment firm holding the account and ask for this information. They should refer back to this information when making withdrawals so they can specify the PSE–EAP breakdown.

ARTISTS, ATHLETES AND OTHER NON-ACADEMIC TYPES

There are several career paths you might take after high school that don't involve college, university or other post-secondary schools approved for RESP use. Also, life doesn't always work out as planned. Suffice it to say there are cases where RESPs that were diligently tended over the years aren't, in the end, needed. Let's look at how your parents can retrieve as much money as possible in such a situation.

An obvious solution here may be to transfer the assets in the unused RESP account to a younger sibling who is either part of the same family plan or has his or her own individual plan. One thing to watch for here is the total amount of Canada Education Savings Grant that a younger sibling ends up with. The limit is $7,200 per person, and any extra will have to be repaid to the government.

If there's no option to transfer RESP assets to a sibling, your parents shouldn't rush to shut the plan down. RESPs can be kept going until the end of the thirty-fifth year after the year in which they were opened. That means your parents can easily wait years to see if there's a change of mind on your part about university or college. If post-secondary schooling becomes a definite no-go, then it's time for your parents to figure out a strategy for collapsing the RESP. Let's look at what happens to the various components of an RESP in this situation. First, there are your parents' contributions over the years. Those are theirs to take back, without penalties or taxes. Next, there's the Canada Education Savings Grant money. That will be returned to the federal government by the financial firm holding the RESP.

Finally, there are the investment gains in the RESP. This money can be taken out of the plan, but your parents will need to wait until you're over 21 years of age and the plan has been in existence for ten years. Parents will have the investment gains pulled from an RESP added to their taxable income, and then they'll have to pay an additional tax of 20 per cent. It's not hard to imagine more than 50 per cent of the investment gains in an RESP—this is called the accumulated income amount—being snapped up by the taxman.

A way around this is for parents to transfer the accumulated income amount to their registered retirement savings plan. There's a $50,000 limit on such transfers, and they'll need to have a matching amount of unused contribution room in their RRSP or a spouse's plan. It's worth noting that once an accumulated income amount is transferred into an RRSP, it can be withdrawn without paying the 20 per cent penalty mentioned earlier. Only income tax at the regular rate applies.

FURTHER READING

Try *The RESP Book: The Complete Guide to Registered Education Savings Plans for Canadians*, by Mike Holman. It covers all arcane RESP rules thoroughly and clearly, and it was written by one of Canada's better personal finance bloggers. Follow Holman at MoneySmartsBlog.com.

FINDING FINANCIAL HELP THROUGH SCHOLARSHIPS

Never assume scholarships are out of reach. True, most are offered on the basis of what's described as *merit*, a term that essentially means high marks. But there are also scholarships awarded on the basis of need, athletic ability and other factors. There's a central clearinghouse of scholarships on a website called Studentawards.com, which describes its mission as follows: "We help you find money for school."

Studentawards.com says its bilingual database contains scholarships that, in total, are worth $70 million. Sign up for the site and you get a personalized list of scholarships, grants and awards that pay anywhere from $500 to $70,000. Studentawards.com is a free service—it makes money by connecting companies and organizations with students for marketing purposes, by administering scholarships and by conducting market research.

Be sure to also check out scholarships and bursaries offered by the school you attend. Some have bursaries worth $100 to $500 for students who achieve a certain mark threshold.

THINKING AHEAD TO UNIVERSITY

As I write this, my 17-year-old son is looking for a part-time job. When he finds one and starts getting paid regularly, I am going to suggest—actually, insist—that he take a small percentage of each paycheque and put it into a savings fund for college or university. The same will apply to his summer jobs. I want him to understand early on what it's like to make sacrifices in order to afford a major expense in the future.

Academically, planning for college and university begins in Grade 11. As you start to examine the options available for your post-secondary education, keep costs uppermost in your mind. For example, attending a school out of town means not only room-and-board expenses, but also the travelling costs of coming home for holidays. For each school on your list, find out the tuition fees and cost of residence, if applicable. Then look at the savings you and your parents have built up and see how much money may need to be borrowed through student loans. Take things a step further by seeing what it would be like to pay back the amount you might have to borrow after you graduate. (You'll find useful student loan calculators on the federal government's CanLearn website at canlearn.ca.)

CONSIDER THE GAP YEAR

Long accepted in Europe, the practice of taking a year off between the end of high school and the beginning of college or university is gaining popularity in Canada for a couple of reasons. One, 17 or 18 is a very young age to switch from the familiar and comfortable experience of high school to the career-specific, more demanding post-secondary path. Two, taking a year off allows both you and your parents to top up your savings and improve your ability to afford the tremendous costs of a post-secondary degree.

High school grads may resist taking a year off because they're uncomfortable with the idea of falling behind friends who are excitedly moving on to the next stage of their lives. For your parents, the worry is that you will spend a year slacking off. Or worse, that you will never go to university or college and thus run the risk of being stuck in a soul-destroying, dead-end job.

In addition to providing you extra time to save, a gap year offers a chance for you to broaden your life experience by working and travelling. You may end up heading to university with a much clearer idea of what you want to do with your life and the level of commitment you'll need to make it happen. If you're seriously considering taking a gap year, tell your parents not to worry that you'll end up with a career "in retail." Experts say that if someone has any aspiration of a lifestyle that includes raising a family, travelling and owning a home and a car, he or she will eventually realize that a post-secondary degree is almost essential.

Don't overlook the potential for a gap year to prevent money being wasted on a failed flirtation with college or university. Better to take some time to figure out what you want to do with your life than to blow $10,000 to $20,000 on a year of school that ends with you dropping out.

As much as a gap year can make financial and emotional sense, there's potential for friction with your parents over whether the time is being well spent. It seems pretty obvious to me that a job would have to be a significant part of your gap-year activities. Some of the money earned could be set aside for education costs later, and some could be used for travel or other activities that broaden your life experience. The guiding principle should be: What can you do in a gap year that will add value to your life?

THOUGHTS ON WHAT TO STUDY

If a college or university degree is an investment, then think about what kind of payoff, or return, you expect for your money. In other words, what kind of career will your degree prepare you for, what kind of an income can you expect and how hard is it to find an entry-level position? This kind of analysis is all the more essential when you're going to borrow significant amounts of money to pay your tuition and expenses.

Here's an idea for doing a cold-eyed assessment of the economic value of the money you'll be spending on college or university. It's from a U.S. student financial aid expert named Mark Kantrowitz, who runs a student aid website (finaid.org). His take is that you should total up the annual cost of your program, multiply it by the number of years you'll need to get your degree and then compare this amount to the starting salary in the field you hope to enter. If the starting salary is lower, give some thought to changing your course of study or finding a cheaper way to get the same degree (e.g., live at home and attend a school in your hometown). My own addition to this analysis is to leave out living expenses and focus only on educational costs. Otherwise, the only jobs that will make the grade are corporate CEO or movie star.

WHAT IT *REALLY* COSTS TO ATTEND COLLEGE OR UNIVERSITY

Thanks to survey work by the people at Studentawards.com, we have a clear picture of what students spend money on and how much they spend. Here's a budget based on a survey of five thousand students. Note: The school year runs from September through at least part of April, so figure on these monthly costs stretching over eight months. And remember, the cost of tuition is not included here.

EXPENSE	(AVG $ PER MONTH)	
	COLLEGE	UNIVERSITY
Rent	$420.30	$457.50
Food and non-alcoholic beverages	$225.50	$225.50
Transportation	$153.50	$122.60
Supplies (personal care, school-related)	$80.70	$71.10
Clothing	$69.20	$61.20
Entertainment	$43.40	$42.90
Alcohol and tobacco	$35.70	$29.50
Total average monthly spending	$1,111.40	$1,080.20

(source: studentawards.com)

I ran these numbers by Zach Dayler, national director at the Canadian Alliance of Student Associations, and he said you should figure on paying $600 to $800 per month if you want to live by yourself as opposed to having a roommate. He also noted that the cost of bus passes may be included in student fees. He's also skeptical about spending in the low-$40 range on monthly entertainment: "Honest, this won't even get you to the bar."

THE STUDENT'S DILEMMA: SHOULD YOU STAY OR SHOULD YOU GO?

Most of the high school graduates I come across have ambitions of going to college or university in another city. It's about independence as much as it is about getting the best possible education, and that's fair. But there's also a major financial component to this question.

As you can see from the budget on the previous page, it costs a lot of money to live away from home. You may have to borrow a significant amount of money to afford it. In the here and now, when you're resigned to borrowing money to afford school, that may not seem like a big deal. But when you graduate and start repaying your loans, the money you borrowed to live away is going to weigh heavily on your lifestyle. After graduation, you may find yourself set back several years in furnishing your apartment, starting your retirement savings, building a business or a hundred other things.

Don't take this as an argument to attend college or university in your hometown and live with your parents. Just ask yourself this if you're considering an out-of-town school: Is the program I want to take going to help make me more successful or give me an edge in building my career? If the answer is yes, then you've got a good argument for attending that out-of-town school. One further thought on going away to school: you may end up spending less if you go to a school in small town, where there are no big-city temptations.

STUDENT BORROWING BASICS

The term *student loan* generally refers to loans obtained through the Canada Student Loans Program, through which the federal government partners with the provinces. Banks also lend money to students, both loans and through student lines of credit. A loan puts a sum of money directly in your hands, while a line of credit sets aside an amount of money that you dip into only as needed. No interest is charged on the line of credit until you withdraw money.

Universities and colleges offer resources to guide students through the application process for government loans, which differs from province to province, and high schools should be able to offer some help as well. Some general points about government student loans:

- They are designed to supplement a family's own savings for post-secondary educational costs, not to be a sole source of funding.
- Applications are assessed on the basis of financial need—if your parents are well off, you may not qualify for government loans.
- Applicants must be Canadian citizens.
- You must be enrolled in a program that runs for at least twelve weeks in a fifteen-week period and is offered by a designated post-secondary institution.
- Full-time students must take at least 60 per cent of a full course load, and part-time students must take between 20 and 59 per cent of a full course load.
- Eligibility for federal and provincial grant money (which

does not need to be paid back) is automatically considered through a student loan application.

- Satisfactory grades must be maintained to continue receiving loan money.
- Applications are submitted through provincial/territorial student loan agencies.

Provincial and territorial contacts for information on student loans: www.canlearn.ca/eng/main/help/contact/cao.shtml

Government student loans are the preferred option for student borrowing. Unlike governments, banks start charging interest on loans as soon as the money is paid to the student. Banks are also less flexible if you need to delay repayment or make special arrangements. The bank line of credit allows you to withdraw only what you need up to an approved credit limit. Once a withdrawal is made, you must make minimum monthly payments (typically just interest, with repayment of the principal delayed until after graduation).

HOTLIST:
TIPS FOR SAVING MONEY IN YOUR STUDENT YEARS

- **Rent your textbooks.** Online services like BookMob (bookmob.ca) and BigMama (bigmama.ca) will ship textbooks for you to use and then return. Much cheaper than buying. To see if your college or university has a textbook rental program, try the directory on efollett (www.bkstr.com).

- **Don't study at Starbucks.** Parking yourself at a coffee chop or pub puts you in the way of temptation to buy stuff. Head to the library instead.
- **Drink and smoke less.** Chill out as required, but mind the cost. Drinking at home is cheaper than going out to a pub.
- **Avoid ATM fees.** Using no-name automated teller machines will cost you between $1.50 and $3 per hit, and the same applies if you use ATMs provided by banks where you don't have an account. Think ahead and always use your bank's ATMs, or use your debit card when you buy things. You'll find more information on banking in Chapter Three.
- **Use Skype to call home.** You'll pay little or nothing to use this online service that connects computers and replaces phones.
- **Look for free events.** Campus movie screenings and free concerts, for example.
- **Bikes and buses rule.** Having a car while you're in college or university is a huge expense to manage without parental assistance. Living near campus will help if you don't have your own wheels.
- **Bank online.** By checking your account frequently, you'll have a good idea of how much money you've got to work with at any given time.

IT'S PAYBACK TIME

Here's a hypothetical example of the mechanics of paying back a $25,000 student loan after graduation. An assumption here is that you will take ten years to repay the loan, including a six-month grace period of no payments after finishing school.

Interest rate	5.5%
Interest built up during the grace period	$687.50
Total amount to be paid back	$25,687.50
Amount of each monthly payment	$289.80
Total interest to be paid over the life of the loan	$7,350.13
Total amount payable	$33,037.63

Source: Canlearn.ca

You'll quickly grasp how heavy a load this is to carry in your first years in the workforce. It's worth reinforcing that this is a ten-year payback schedule. Squeeze the term down to six years, including grace period, and the monthly payments rise to something in the area of $420. Are your parents willing to do as much as they reasonably can to avoid your carrying a debt load like this? Then make sure they're hip to the benefits of the registered education savings plan, or RESP.

HOW PAYING BACK STUDENT DEBT WORKS

The loans you took out to pay for university may seem like a curse when you're still repaying them years after graduation and would love to put the money toward something else. But in one way, a student loan is the sweetest deal you're ever going to get when borrowing money. Understanding exactly how these loans work will help you become debt-free sooner and become a smarter borrower when you take on a mortgage, a car loan or a line of credit later in life.

A key question when borrowing money for any purpose is: What are the rules for paying it back? When you borrow money through a government-run student loan program, the rules are totally slack by real-world standards, in that you're not charged interest until you graduate, take a break of longer than six months from your studies or drop out. In the real world, interest starts building up on a loan instantly. With student loans, your money is basically cost-free until graduation.

As a graduating student, you get a breather of up to six months before you have to start paying back your student loan. It's called a grace period, and it's designed to give you time to find a job and start drawing a paycheque. What could possibly be wrong with taking a breather like this?

A little something called interest, which is how banks and other lenders make money by providing loans. All through your grace period, interest is growing on the amount you owe the government in student loans. As you can see in the example above, hundreds of dollars in interest costs can build up through the grace period. You can pay this interest off in a lump sum once the grace period is over—that's the preferred solution—or you can have the interest added to the total amount you owe. Although most people end up doing the latter, it's the worst approach because interest will now be applied not only to the total amount of your student loans, but also to the interest bill you racked up during the grace period. In other words, you'll be paying interest on interest.

As you go through life, you'll find this type of choice facing you more than a few times. Quick example: your bank may invite you to skip a mortgage payment with absolutely no hassle, possibly around the holiday season. If you do, then the interest you would have paid off with the skipped mortgage payment (with all payments, you pay some interest and some principal, a term that refers to the amount you borrowed) will be added to the total amount you've paid on your mortgage. Again, you'll be paying interest on interest.

TIP: If you've taken advantage of the six-month grace period to repay your loans and then landed a job before the six months are up, start attacking your student loan right away rather than waiting.

Upon finishing school, your loan provider will attempt to contact you. Note: In some provinces, you will have to pay back separate loans to the provincial and federal governments, while in others payments are made only to the province. So verify how many loans you have to pay back, and to whom you'll be making payments. Then make it clear whether you're going to take advantage of the six-month grace period.

Notification of the details of your loan repayment will arrive by mail. You'll be told the total amount of your loan, the interest rate on the loan, the monthly amount that will be taken out of your bank account, the date withdrawals will occur each month and the length of time it will take to fully repay the loan. If you don't hear from the student loan authorities, contact them. Believe me, they haven't forgotten about you.

Here's a key lesson about life that is taught by student loans: it's ultimately up to you to ensure you repay what you owe. No one is going to put sticky notes on the fridge door or nag you to make sure you're on top of things. What happens if you ignore your student debts? After your six-month grace period is up, it's possible that monthly payments will automatically start being withdrawn from the bank account to which your student loan money was deposited (assuming you arranged for direct deposit). If you're not on top of things, you may default on your payments and thereby hurt your credit rating. This in turn could impair your ability later on to get a credit card, mortgage or car loan.

A STUDENT'S GUIDE TO INTEREST RATES AND BORROWING COSTS

Among the decisions to make at the time you arrange repayment of your student loan is the interest rate on your debt. You have two choices:

- A fixed rate of prime + 5% (prime is the base lending rate the banks reserve for top customers)
- A floating rate of prime + 2.5%

Here, again, is a financial lesson taught by student loans. With a fixed-rate loan, you have the certainty of knowing your borrowing costs are locked in and will never change, no matter what's happening in the economy or how high interest rates rise. But you pay for that assurance through an interest rate that is 5 percentage points more than prime, compared to 2.5 points higher for a floating-rate loan. The catch for getting the lower rate is that you're vulnerable to rising debt charges. In setting their prime rates, the banks take direction from the Bank of Canada, which constantly monitors the economy to evaluate whether interest rates should remain steady, be increased to cool overheated economic growth or be lowered to stimulate a struggling economy.

If the Bank of Canada raises rates, the banks will in turn increase their prime rates and you will in turn face higher rates on your student loan. It's quite possible you could sign up for a floating-rate student loan and then watch as the prime rate rises 2.5 percentage points and puts you on the same footing as the fixed-rate people. And then prime could move still higher, putting you at a disadvantage. The net effect of rising rates is more interest to be repaid, which in turn could make it take longer to kill off your debt.

Later on in life, when you're buying a home, you'll face a similar decision about whether to go with a fixed- or floating-rate mortgage. At that point, you'll probably come across this advice: go with your gut. If the threat of rising interest rates will weigh on you, then go with a fixed rate. You'll probably also come across a reference to studies showing that floating-rate loans have in the past been cheaper in most but not all cases. The reason is that rates usually move higher in a slow, measured way that extends the benefit you're getting from your floating-rate loan being cheaper to start with than the fixed-rate loan. Also, when rates do move a lot higher, they don't tend to say that way for long. My take: go with a cheaper floating-rate loan, unless you're a worrier.

> **TAX TIP:**
> Students repaying government student loans should remember that there is a tax credit on the interest portion of their payments. If you can't use the credit because your income is zero, save it for use over the next five years. Note: The credit applies even if someone else is paying the loan interest for you.

SORRY TO NAG, BUT . . .

It's worth repeating: if graduates do nothing about their loans, the matter will be referred to a debt collection agency and they will have a black mark added to their credit bureau file. That could make it hard to get a loan or mortgage later on, and put them in the acutely embarrassing situation of being chased by bill collectors.

There are resources available to help you if you can't make your payments on schedule. Through the Repayment Assistance Program, you may be able to arrange temporarily lower payments that are better suited to your income level. If you remember one thing about student loans, let it be that they're your introduction to the adult world of money. Handle your loans like an adult and you'll build the skills for a lifetime of responsible borrowing. Let your loans slide and you may find that you're still being punished for it years into the future.

THE DEBT TRAP: HOW PARENTS CAN HELP

Parents can help kids loaded down with student debt by simply paying off or paying down the loan. But there's another option that doesn't completely absolve the student of all responsibility for dealing with his or her debts. Here's how it works: First, the parents pay off the loan in full or in part. Then they work out a personalized repayment plan that can include all kinds of variations. I've heard of arrangements where the parents take 50 per cent of their son's or daughter's debt repayments and insist that the other 50 per cent go into a registered retirement savings plan or tax-free savings account.

Other potential arrangements include parents having their kids postpone repayment until they land a good job or having them direct the debt repayments in a savings plan for a down payment on a house.

TAX TIPS FOR STUDENTS

Let's get right to the good news here. It's unlikely that students will have to pay any income tax on money they earn through part-time work or receive through RESPs set up by their parents. For one thing, Canadians in 2011 were allowed to have taxable income of $10,527 annually without paying federal tax (this is called the basic personal amount, and it's indexed to inflation). It's possible that provincial taxes may apply at this income level, but only a tiny amount.

Another reason why students are unlikely to pay tax is the range of tax savings for which they're eligible. Here's a quick summary compiled by Jamie Golombek, tax and estate planning expert at Canadian Imperial Bank of Commerce:

- **Moving expenses.** Claimable by students who move more than 40 kilometres from home to attend school, or accept a new job, say, in the summer or after graduation. The deduction is limited by employment income in case of accepting a job.
- **Tuition, education and textbook tax credits.** If these credits aren't needed to lower a student's tax bill to zero, up to $5,000 annually can be transferred to parents, or any unused amounts carried forward for you to use in another year.
- **Interest on student loans.** A credit is available for interest paid on government student loans. It can be carried forward for up to five years if you don't need it currently.
- **Public transit passes.** A tax credit is available to people who buy monthly passes.

Golombek notes that students are under no obligation to file a return if they do not owe taxes. Still, he points out a few good reasons for doing so. One is that filing a tax return may enable a student with a part-time job to receive a refund of taxes deducted from his or her paycheques by an employer. Another is that filing a tax return allows a student to start building up contribution room for registered retirement savings plans that can be used later. RRSP room is calculated at 18 per cent of the previous year's earned income, which is basically employment income.

Students who are 19 or older have an additional reason

to file a tax return. (Note: You may be able to get help with tax filing on campus.) By doing so, they make themselves eligible to receive a GST/HST tax credit, which is paid each quarter to people with lower incomes to help cover the goods and services tax or harmonized sales tax they pay.

Here's a handy calculator for students, or anyone else, to calculate the taxes they'll owe: www.theglobeandmail. com/globe-investor/personal-finance/investing-calculators/ calculate-your-tax-bill/article1731948/?from=1974904

ONLINE TOOLS FOR STUDENTS

- **Canlearn.ca.** A federal government website with details on all aspects of funding your post-secondary education.
- **Student Finance 101 (www.debt101.ca).** A nonprofit website set up as a financial resource for students.
- **Studentawards.com.** A directory of scholarships and bursaries available to students.
- **Bank websites for students** (mind the sales pitches here).

    TD Canada Trust: www.tdcanadatrust.com/student/smartsaving.jsp

    Bank of Nova Scotia: www.fundyourfuture.ca/manageyourmoney/

    manageyourmoney.aspx

    CIBC: www.cibc.com/ca/student-life/

    Royal Bank: www.betterstudentlife.ca/

    Bank of Montreal: www.bmo.com/smartstepsportal/student/en/

CHAPTER ONE SUMMARY

1. RESPs rule. Unless your parents are okay with you being loaded down like a mule with student debt, they should be paying as much attention to registered education

savings plans as to tax-free savings accounts and registered retirement savings plans; if cash is in short supply
and your parents can't swing an RESP, then student
loans are your backstop.

2. **Scholarships are out there.** Good marks are certainly a way
to earn a scholarship, but they're not the only way.

3. **Borrow if necessary, but don't necessarily borrow.** Paying off
student loans will affect your ability to buy a car, a
home and other adult stuff.

4. **Pay attention when payback time comes.** Neglecting your
student loans can ruin your credit rating, which can make
it hard to find someone to lend you money later in life.

5. **File a tax return.** Students likely won't have to pay any
income taxes, but there are benefits to filing a tax
return anyway.

CASE STUDY: Stephen

Note: Several case studies are presented in this book so
that you can learn from the financial experience of real
people attending university, entering the workforce and
buying homes. Each case study is a snapshot of where an
individual was at the time this book was being written.

Stephen, 21, has been pursuing a commerce degree at
St. Mary's University in Halifax. Through a mix of his
own savings, help from his parents and scholarships,
he's managed to live in residence and limit his student
loans to $12,000. Let's look closer at how Stephen has
managed things.

Annual cost of tuition: $5,580.

Estimated cost of other educational expenses: $2,000.

Estimated annual living costs: $19,880.

Primary source of funds to cover tuition, expenses: Student loans, parents, summer employment.

Total amount borrowed so far: $12,000.

Anticipated future amount he will need to borrow: $0.

Financial help from parents? Yes, about $40,000.

Amount saved himself through jobs, gifts, etc.: $20,000.

Anything his parents could have done to make university/college more financially manageable for him? Nothing. They were spectacular.

Scholarship or bursary? I had a scholarship worth $3,500 for three of my four years.

Worst financial mistake made so far with respect to post-secondary education: I started investing in March 2008 and lost 27 per cent right off the bat.

Smartest financial moves with respect to post-secondary education: Claiming the tax credits that students are eligible for, and opening a tax-free savings account.

Advice for other students on managing finances while in college or university: Get a good job—internships, co-ops, government positions, things you like. Build experience while making good money. Also, don't drink too much. (I've heard of people spending hundreds of dollars in one night. Don't be that guy.) And don't sign up for credit cards with high spending limits. Do not put your spring break vacation on your credit card. (Again, I have seen people do this.) Quite simply, do not spend exorbitant amounts of money on anything.

Part-time job? No.

Do you have a credit card in your name? Yes.

How easy was it to get the card? Really, really, really easy. Granted, I was also opening an investment account the same day, so they were probably reassured that I knew a thing or two about money management.

Do you use your credit often, or just for emergences? Often. Online purchases are a large part of how I buy things.

Do you pay in full each month you use the card, or are you running a balance? In full every month, without fail.

Have you ever skipped a payment because you couldn't afford it? No.

TWO

HOW TO HANDLE DEBT, BOTH IN SCHOOL AND AFTERWARD

Shrewd handling of credit is one of the things that define a financially successful person. It's arguably more important than making smart investments, being a good bargain hunter or anything else. Now, let's not get all puritanical here and act like debt is evil and must be resisted at all costs. Debt is a tool—it can help you reach financial goals like completing a post-secondary education or buying a home, and it can help you achieve lifestyle aspirations like buying a car. But you have to control debt, or it will burn you.

It's surprisingly easy to borrow more than you can afford to pay back. You can do it with a credit card or a line of credit. You keep making minimum payments each month while running up the balance with new purchases. Pretty soon, your debts are so big you can't afford to carry them any longer, never mind pay them down. Worst case, you blow out your credit rating or even declare bankruptcy. These risks are well known, and yet we still live in a world where many people routinely fail to pay off their credit card balances in full at the end of every month. In other words, they're living beyond their means.

First lesson on borrowing: distinguish between good and bad debt. Good debt has the net effect of adding to your personal wealth or earning power. A student loan that helps you earn a useful degree and build a career is a great example of good debt. Bad debt refers to borrowing for things you can't really afford and should deny yourself until you can afford them. This consumption-crazed society we live in makes it tough to keep a lid on spending, but self-control is the first step to being a smart borrower.

WHERE BAD ATTITUDES ABOUT CREDIT BEGIN

Credit cards are a marvel. You present a colourful plastic card to a store clerk, take it back moments later and then walk away with the goods.

It is really as easy at that: credit cards seemingly let you buy stuff for free.

In your dreams, that is. And yet, many people who understand that things bought on plastic aren't actually free can be lulled into thinking that repayment isn't really important, or that it can be delayed.

I'm not just talking about young people. You're not the ones who built up today's high levels of personal debt in relation to income. That distinction belongs to older

Canadians, many of them parents who are setting examples for their children.

Faulty thinking about debt among young adults is apparent in the results of a survey of 3,079 young adults aged 18 to 34 that was conducted by researchers at Ohio State University. A bizarre finding of this survey: among 18- to 28-year-olds, the more they owed in student loans and credit card debt, the more self-esteem they felt from the indebtedness. "Young people seem to view debt mostly in just positive terms rather than as a potential burden," the authors of the study found. They expected that young adults might have a positive view of student loans because they're arguably a way for someone to invest in his or her future. But they also thought—wrongly, as it turned out—that there would be a negative take on credit card debt.

Interestingly, students from less-well-off families felt more self-esteem as a result of their debts, while students from affluent families got no boost at all. Debt as self-actualization? Wake up, people. Debt, at its worst, is a form of penal servitude.

WAYS PARENTS CAN RAISE FINANCIALLY SMART KIDS
If you have younger siblings, your parents can apply these tips to them. Or use them with your own children.

- **Give kids an allowance.** It's up to the parent how much to pay and whether to link the allowance to chores. The important lesson is how to handle money—spend some, save some, and if you're so inclined, give some to charity.

- **Pay kids for special assignments around the house.** The allowance is to cover day-to-day chores. For big jobs like cleaning up the basement or weeding the entire lawn, reward them in a way that teaches entrepreneurialism (more initiative, more reward).
- **Open a bank account for them.** An ideal way to reinforce how saving money works. Make sure the account has online access so it's possible to keep track of how the savings are mounting up (forget about bankbooks—they're so yesterday). Note: There's more information on kiddie accounts in Chapter Three.
- **Teach them the good and the bad of interest.** The good is that you make money on your savings (not much, but some); the bad is the cost of borrowing money.
- **Encourage goals.** Whether it's for a toy or an iPad, gradually saving for the things you want is an important life skill.
- **Explain family decisions in the context of cost.** "Yes, it would be nice to go out for dinner, but we don't want to spend money on that right now," or "Disneyland would be a great family vacation, but it's going to take us a year to save up the money to go."
- **Explain how taxes work.** Use a pay stub to show how some of your earnings are taken by the government to pay for things like highways, hospitals, airports, libraries, hockey arenas and so forth. Let kids make up their own minds about whether taxes are fair.
- **Involve kids in family financial decision-making.** Should you buy a big-screen TV or go to Florida at March break?
- **Teach advertising savvy.** Point out how ads create demand

for products we didn't know we needed, and in fact, do not at all need.

- **Let kids feel the no-money pinch.** Not being able to afford something you really, really want is part of life. The best lessons come from situations where a child can't buy what he or she wants because of previous bad spending decisions.
- **Teach smart shopping habits.** Waiting for sales, using coupons, buying online.
- **Keep an eye on your kids' employment income.** When your child is old enough to get a part-time job, suggest that he or she have two bank accounts, one for saving up for things he or she wants and one for day-to-day spending. You might also suggest putting a bit aside each payday for university or college.

THE SCANDAL OF STUDENT CREDIT CARDS

Lesson number one about handling credit is that banks will give you a credit card without any certainty that you can pay what you owe. In fact, banks don't just give students cards—they actively promote the idea of students having them. Every bank's website has a page on cards for students. Card applications are easily found on campus—I remember this from when I attended university all the way back in the mid-1980s. I can also recall a big bank setting up a credit card kiosk aimed at students in Toronto's massive downtown Eaton Centre mall one recent summer.

Credit card applications for students should be done up like cigarette packages—*This product can kill you financially, so be careful.* Instead, they talk about benefits like earning points or the availability one type of insurance coverage or another. Those are important features if you're a well-employed person looking for a credit card, but they're largely irrelevant to the student who has no income to speak of.

As we saw in the previous chapter, students graduate with an average debt of more than $25,000. Do all you can to avoid adding to this amount with a credit card balance that follows you all through university.

Let's look at how easy it is to get a card as a student, using the example of one particular bank. On the bank's website, it says that you need to be enrolled full time at a recognized college or university, and have a minimum income of $1,200 per year, to qualify for a Visa card for students. From a financial point of view, the bank might just as well say you can get one of its Visa cards if you're a student and you have a pulse. In the real world, $1,200 year, or $100 per month, isn't close to enough to allow you to manage a credit card plus the other expenses of student life.

Say you successfully apply for one of these credit cards, and then you run up a balance beyond what you can pay back when the bill comes. Now we come to lesson number two about handling credit, which is that interest will smother you if you don't watch out. The aforementioned Visa card carried a rate, as this book was being written, of 19.99 per cent, which is typical for a card of its type. If you can't pay your balance in full by the due date, then interest starts applying.

The minimum required payment for student credit cards tends to be 2 to 3 per cent of your outstanding card balance, or $10, whichever is larger. If you paid the minimum every month (the minimum amount will decline as you pay down the balance) on a $1,000 balance, it would take you almost eleven years to get your card paid off. The total interest bill would be $989.53. That's an extreme example, so let's see what happens if you pay off $100 per month. Here, it takes you a year to get the balance down to zero, with a total interest cost of $102.99.

There are a few small pluses to student credit cards. One, they tend not to have annual fees, and two, they usually have very low credit limits of $300 to $1,000. Compared to the damage these cards can do, such benefits are insignificant.

The bottom line on student credit cards is to know yourself. Can you handle the card responsibly, or is there a risk that you'll misuse it and start racking up debt you cannot afford to pay back? If you see any risk at all, then wait to get a credit card until you have the job and salary you'll need to use it properly.

STUDENT CREDIT CARD RUNDOWN

The Financial Consumer Agency of Canada offers a regularly updated summary of all types of credit cards, including student cards. Here are some characteristics of student cards:

- **Minimum income needed to qualify.** Most cards do not specify an amount, while others range as high as $1,200.
- **Credit limits.** Between $300 and $1,000.

- **Minimum payments.** Typically 2 to 3 per cent of the out-standing balance, or $10.
- **Annual fees.** Usually zero, although low-rate cards for students can cost $35.
- **Interest rates.** In the 19 per cent range for regular cards and in 12 to 13 per cent range for low-rate cards.

More info: www.fcac-acfc.gc.ca/eng/default.asp.

CREDIT CARDS: ONE FAMILY'S STORY

A reader of my *Globe and Mail* column has emailed me a few times to update me on his daughter's nightmarish adventure with credit cards. Attending university, and with only a part-time job, this young woman was granted a credit card by one of the big banks. Before long, she had racked up $500 in debt on the card and was missing payments.

"I was noticing how nervous she always was when the mail came, and she would bolt to the door to get it," the father recalled. "Well, I got one letter and had her open it for me and it was from the collection agency." He paid the bill and had his daughter do some chores around the house to pay the money back.

This was not the end of the story. Several months later, another collection agency letter arrived at the house, this one for a $1,261 debt on another bank credit card that the daughter had obtained earlier, when she was all of 19 years old. After negotiating the debt down to $1,000, he paid it off and emailed me to offer a lesson for other parents: don't let your kids sign up for credit cards before they can afford them. "Put the word out," he wrote. "I'll bet there are thousands of parents like me out there."

SHOULD YOUR PARENTS GIVE YOU A CREDIT CARD FOR EMERGENCIES?

You're moving away from home and your parents are worried about what you will do if a sudden and sizable expense comes up. An easy solution is to get an additional card added to their account and give it you. Just for emergencies, of course.

If your parents want to infantilize you, they should most definitely follow up on this plan. They'll be teaching the lesson that come what may in the world, Mommy and Daddy will always bail you out. Just pull out the magic credit card and your financial problems are gone.

There are two alternative approaches to covering off the very real possibility that while attending university or college, you'll need an emergency cash infusion for very legit purposes (for example, if your laptop is fried). One is for your parents to transfer cash directly from their bank account to your account using PayPal or an Interac e-Transfer (details in Chapter Three). Once you accept the Interac e-Transfer, the money is instantly available in your account, provided you deal with a participating bank. If not, it can take a few days for your money to arrive.

Another alternative is offered up with a giant-size warning because it may very well result in major frustration for both you and your parents. We're talking here about credit cards that are preloaded with money and usable anywhere credit is accepted as payment for goods and services. There are two types of card in this category.

The non-reloadable gift card. You'll find these sold in drug stores, grocery stores and other outlets. Some banks may also offer them. Gift credit cards typically come in denominations ranging from $25 to $200 or even $500. On top of the face-value amount, expect to pay an additional $3.95 to $6.95 or so to activate the card. No name appears on the card, so anyone of any age can use one.

In theory, these cards are a super option as a portable emergency fund while you're away at university or college or travelling. In practice, they can be a minefield of fees that will blow you away. There can be monthly maintenance fees, replacement fees for lost cards (register a card and you'll be able to retain the unused value if it's lost) and expiry fees that eat up any remaining unspent balance on the card. Note: You can register the card and view your balance online.

As a general rule, you should expect to have six months of use from the card before monthly maintenance fees of $1.50 to $2.50 or so start kicking in. So if you buy one in September, you might at worst have to pay $5 or so in monthly fees before the end of the academic year. Avoid the sheer robbery of the expiry fee by ensuring that a card will last through the academic year. You'll find the expiry date on the front of the card. If you haven't used up the card as the expiry date approaches, be sure to spend the balance down to the last penny. Note: As this book was written, gift cards issued by American Express Canada had no monthly fees, no expiration fee and could be replaced for free.

You may be aware that store-issued gift cards can be covered by provincial legislation that prevents them from ever expiring. As this book was written, gift cards issued by credit card companies were not covered.

The reloadable prepaid credit card. Available through a small number of banks and credit unions, reloadable cards are problematic because they'll typically need to have a parent's name embossed on the front. Bank of Montreal offers a way around this with its Prepaid Travel MasterCard, which can be loaded with between $100 and $10,000. Your parents will need to buy one of these cards for $9.95—it's very handy for travel—and then buy an additional supplementary card for you for another $9.95 (both valid for three years). The supplementary card will be in your name and can be used in all the usual credit card ways, including for cash advances. Need to have some money added to your card? Your parents can do it online, like a bill payment, through most big banks, and the money will be transferred in two to five business days.

The BMO card expires after three years, though you can get any balance remaining refunded to you, minus any applicable fees. Also, this card can charge inactivity fees, but it does not charge monthly maintenance fees as some other reloadable prepaid credit cards do.

With their fees and conditions, prepaid gift cards and reloadable cards have been justifiably criticized by many people, including parents who have bought them for their kids. Used carefully, though, these cards are a useful financial training tool because they put you in charge of your own emergency fund.

DEBT IS NOT A SWEAR WORD

One of the oddities of the last recession was the way many Canadians continued to borrow money despite economic uncertainty and rising job losses. The reason was obvious: interest rates fell to levels so low that people couldn't resist taking out mortgages and running up their lines of credit. Eventually, debt levels rose to a point where the governor of the Bank of Canada—call him the person ultimately responsible for running the economy—issued warnings to people about reducing the amount they owed. His message was on the money. Debts that seem manageable when interest rates are low can become overwhelming when rates move up, as they always do when the economy grows.

A lot of people ignored the debt warnings, but others took to bad-mouthing debt as some sort of weakness of character displayed by people who cannot deny themselves things that are out of their price range. This is nonsense. Debt is an essential tool for living your life in a society where a house can easily cost five to ten times a young adult's starting salary in the workforce. Save up for a home so you can pay in cash? With big-city housing prices where they are these days, the only home you'll make it into will be a retirement home.

HOW TO BUILD A GOOD CREDIT RATING

As soon as you land a decent-paying job upon graduation, you should start trying to establish yourself as a good borrower and thereby build a high credit score as tallied by the major credit bureaus.

These credit bureaus—Equifax and TransUnion are the

big names—operate in the background, and many people are unaware they exist. Even so, the information kept by credit bureaus is all-powerful when it comes to a bank or other lender's decision about whether to lend you money. Credit bureaus gather information on how people manage their debts and then convert it into credit scores. If you apply for a loan or a mortgage, the lender will ask for your permission to view your credit score and other information in your file. Will you get the loan you want? Will you need a co-signer? What interest rate will be charged? These questions are answered in large part by what's in your credit file.

By the way, you should check your credit bureau files periodically, regardless of whether you need to borrow money. Correctible mistakes and outdated information can sometimes find their way into these documents. Also, your credit file will list all the credit cards, loans and lines of credit you have. This may be just the kick in the butt you need to rationalize your credit. Cancel what you never use and don't need, but be mindful that cancelling a card can negatively affect your credit rating. You read that right. The way credit scoring is done, you can actually be penalized for closing a credit card account. This is especially true for cards that you have had for a long period of time.

Where to Go to Order a Copy of Your Credit File
- Equifax: www.consumer.equifax.ca/home/en_ca
- TransUnion: www.transunion.ca/

HOTLIST:
EXPERT TIPS ON BUILDING A SOLID CREDIT RATING

I asked Laurie Campbell, executive director at the nonprofit counselling agency Credit Canada, for some tips to help people who are just starting in the workforce build and maintain a good credit rating. Here's what she came up with:

- **Pay all your bills on time.** Paying late or having your account sent to a collection agency has a negative impact on your credit score.
- **Try not to run your balances up to your credit limit.** Keeping your account balances below 50 per cent of your available credit may also help your score.
- **Avoid applying for credit unless you have a genuine need for a new account.** Too many inquiries in a short period of time can sometimes be interpreted as a sign that you are opening numerous credit accounts owing to financial difficulties or overextending yourself by taking on more debt than you can actually repay. A flurry of inquiries will prompt most lenders to ask you why. However, most scoring formulas will not penalize you if, for example, you are shopping for the best mortgage rate or the best car loan.
- **Limit the number of credit cards you have.** The more credit you have available, the more it appears you could get yourself into financial difficulty.
- **Make sure the most up-to-date and accurate information is on your credit report.** Being listed as a student well after you are out of school could be seen as negative.

- **Don't sign a credit contract until you have read it and understood it.** If you don't understand, ask questions until you are satisfied.
- **Avoid co-signing for family members, friends or acquaintances.** If they fail to pay, you are on the hook for the total debt.
- **Be sure you understand the total cost of your purchases.** Avoid finding yourself in a situation of owing more than you realized you would.
- **Check your credit rating before applying for any major credit.** If there is any incorrect information on your file, it can be corrected before a potential creditor views it.
- **Use credit wisely.** It's for safety, convenience and planned purchases.

Note: Nonprofit credit counselling agencies can be a good place to turn if you feel overwhelmed by debt. They can help you create a budget to pay back what you owe. They can also help you negotiate with your credit card companies and other lenders to reduce interest rates and monthly payments. Two points to consider: fees may be involved if you adopt a debt-repayment program arranged by a credit counselling agency, and your use of such a service can conceivably affect your credit file negatively. This is a point of dispute with the agencies themselves, which argue that using their services can actually help improve your creditworthiness.

INTO THE WORKFORCE

Once you're working, a good way to start building a favourable credit profile is to apply for a credit card. How is it that credit cards were a disaster waiting to happen when you were a student, but they're okay now? Simple—now that you're working and earning an income, you're in a position to manage a credit card properly.

That means using a card as a way to manage the purchase of things you can afford right now but choose not to pay for immediately. Maybe it's a large purchase and you're not carrying enough cash around to pay for it. Or maybe you want to rack up reward points. Either way, the underlying assumption is that you have the cash to pay for what you're buying. You're simply using the credit card as a tool that gives you flexibility in making that purchase.

When you're just starting out in the workforce, a no-fee credit card makes the most sense. There are plenty of reward programs available through no-fee cards, so shop the market carefully and apply for a card that will do something useful for you. Early on, there's no point in trying for an elite gold or platinum card—salary requirements to get one can be high, and the annual fee of $120 or so is prohibitively expensive when viewed against the kind of reward points you're likely to earn based on your spending.

Most banks offer a low-interest card, where the interest rate can be as low as 10 to 15 per cent, instead of the more usual 19 per cent or so. Forget about these cards—having one means you're surrendering to the idea of carrying a balance on your card and will end up paying an exorbitant amount in interest.

Once you've got your credit card, use it strategically to build up a positive credit rating. Make only purchases you are 101 per cent certain to be able to repay on time. Late payments are a credit killer, so be sure to pay your card bill well in advance of the due date. Don't be a dinosaur and pay by mail. Instead, set your credit card as a bill payee on your online banking website. Remember, it can take twenty-four to forty-eight hours for an online payment to be credited to your card account.

CREDIT CARDS: DON'T LEAVE HOME WITHOUT THEM

Let's be honest about credit cards: in today's financial world, they're essential. Without one, you are a second-class citizen who will have all kinds of trouble booking travel (just try securing a hotel room for late arrival or renting a car without one) and buying things online from many retailers. Note: PayPal and online debit through Interac are increasingly becoming options for online payments, though they're far from replacing credit cards.

SHOULD YOU ASK YOUR PARENTS TO CO-SIGN A LOAN?

Let's say you're working full time in a good job and you want to take out a car loan. Though your income is more than sufficient to carry the payments, your bank doesn't want to make the loan. The reason? You lack a credit history, which means you're viewed as a risky bet.

An easy way to make this problem go away is to ask one of your parents to co-sign the loan. Don't do this casually, though. Be certain you're financially solid enough to carry your loan. If you default, your parents will be on the hook. That's just what your folks need—to be carrying your car loan at a time when they'll quite likely want to be ramping up their retirement savings program.

LOAN BASICS

Your first loan, quite possibly for the purchase of a car, will most likely carry a hefty interest rate. Suck it up, build your credit score by making your loan payments on time and then, after a year or two, see what you can do to get the rate on your loan down.

Consumer loans can be paid off anytime with no penalty, which means you can easily move your loan from one lender to another. Let's say you bought a car using dealer financing at an interest rate you were forced to accept because that was the best rate available anywhere, including from your bank. Eighteen months later, you're doing well at work and you've made all your loan payments on time. It's now time to see if you can get a better rate on your car loan. Go back to your bank, and if you don't like what you hear, check some other banks as well.

If you can find a better rate, jump on it. What you'll

GET YOUR LOAN RATE DOWN

Here's how lowering the interest rate on a loan takes money out of your banker's pocket and puts it in yours. We'll assume you're borrowing $15,000 and taking five years to pay it back.

INTEREST RATE	MONTHLY PAYMENT	TOTAL INTEREST
10%	$318.71	$4,122.34
8%	$304.15	$3,248.75
6%	$289.99	$2,399.52
4%	$276.25	$1,574.87

essentially be doing is taking out a new loan and using the proceeds to pay off your old loan. This is an easy procedure—I did it myself with a car loan when I was in my twenties, and I've helped others do the same thing over the years.

Once you're well established in the working world and have built a solid credit history, ask at your bank about an unsecured line of credit for your borrowing. A credit line is like a pre-arranged loan that stands ready for you to use it. You pay interest only when you draw down on your credit line, which will have a maximum amount you can borrow. Credit lines are great for two reasons, but they're also dangerous for weak-willed spenders.

The best thing about credit lines is that interest rates are typically lower than for loans, and vastly lower than for credit cards. The rates are also negotiable, so you'll need to have a chat with your banker. Rates are looked at in terms of how much over the bank's prime lending rate (reserved for top customers) you'll have to pay. Another reason to like credit lines is the flexible repayment schedule. You may have to make a set minimum payment each month, maybe 2 or 3 per cent of what you borrowed, or in many cases you can just pay the interest you owe. Beyond that, it's up to you to decide how quickly to pay back what you owe.

The danger with credit lines should be obvious: the temptation to use them for whimsical reasons that make no financial sense, like clothes and electronics. Some people get used to permanently owing money on their lines of credit, and they even think they're smart because they're paying less interest than they would on a credit card. And yet, they're still living beyond their means.

The best kind of credit line is called the home-equity line of credit—bankers called it a HELOC. Rates are the lowest possible with a HELOC because you have secured the loan with your home. You'll need a home for that, which we'll get to in Chapter Seven.

DEBT AS A WAY OF LIFE

The underlying idea behind what you've been reading here is that debt is part of life and must be intelligently managed. I wouldn't want you to get the idea, however, that debt should be a permanent feature of life.

Unfortunately, that's how a lot of people have come to regard debt. As soon as they've paid off their credit card debts, they use them to buy something else. As soon as they make some headway paying down their mortgages, they move to a bigger house. As you'll read in coming chapters, I'm a big believer in paying off debt to build a strong foundation for saving. But you'll never do that if you keep exchanging one debt for another.

Let's close here with the idea that zero debt is an ideal financial state. We may struggle to get there, but when we do we want to remain there as long as possible.

CHAPTER TWO SUMMARY

1. **Understand the credit card trap.** Resist getting a credit card until you're confident you can handle it. Be honest with yourself.

2. **Build your credit rating.** Borrow carefully so that your credit file tells prospective lenders you're a desirable customer who deserves the best interest rates.

3. **Borrow as cheaply as possible.** Remember that there are various ways to borrow with widely varying interest rates—be sure you're borrowing as cheaply as possible.

CASE STUDY: Jamie

Jamie left her home in Brampton, Ontario, to attend the University of Ottawa, where over seven years she earned a bachelor's degree and then a master's. After finishing her education, she landed a permanent part-time job at an Ottawa social services agency that enabled her to pay off her considerable student loans. Let's see what Jamie, aged 28, learned about paying for school that might be useful to you.

Estimated total cost of tuition: $38,000.

Estimated cost of other educational expenses: $7,000.

Estimated living costs: $84,000 ($12,000 per year).

Primary source of funds to cover tuition, expenses: Student loans, undergrad and graduate scholarships, and income from summer jobs.

Money available from an RESP set up by parents: $0.

Total amount borrowed: $25,500.

Total amount repaid to date: All of it.

Worst financial mistake made so far with respect to post-secondary education: Not looking at other universities that are more generous with their scholarships; not taking time between high school and university to figure out what I was passionate about.

Smartest financial moves related to post-secondary education: Living frugally, maintaining scholarships, paying off credit cards in full and not accruing interest.

Advice for other students on managing finances: Limit number and use of credit cards and pay off your purchases in full before the due date. . . . Think about what you actually *need* (food, toilet paper) and your *wants* (beer, smokes, nice clothes, iPad), and limit *want* purchases.

Biggest financial surprise while in university: The high cost of tuition and living expenses.

Biggest financial stresses when starting in the workforce: Finding a job, paying off student debt and dealing with the high cost of renting. (Jamie said the average apartment rental in her city is $800.)

Starting salary in first job: $35,000 (for four days per week).

Advice for other young adults starting work: Volunteer and network within the community during school years. . . . Many employers hire internally and many definitely support hiring people they are familiar with.

Financial lessons my parents taught me: None. . . . My father is a deadbeat who shirked all parental and financial responsibilities, while my mother is the most financially illiterate and irresponsible person ever.

THREE

YOU AND YOUR BANK

Banks are basically stores that offer financial products for sale. They are in business to sell you stuff, not to be your adviser, your partner or your friend. You may end up having a rewarding relationship with the people at your bank, but never forget who they ultimately work for. It's the bank's shareholders, not you.

This warning is important as you move into university or college and then the workforce, because the relationship you have with your bank is going to change. To start, that rinky-dink little savings account you had as child won't cut it any longer. You'll need a proper chequing account—one that doesn't soak you with fees—and then likely a credit card. Let's begin with your chequing account.

The banking needs of students are simple because, let's

face it, they don't have much money, and what money they do have tends to be spent rather than saved or invested. Fortunately, one of the ways banks have of deflecting criticism about all the fees they charge is to maintain free banking for students (and seniors). Student banking is one of the best financial bargains around, but it doesn't last long.

Once out of school, students are regarded as adults by the banks. With adult bank accounts comes the risk of being subjected not only to a wide array of fees, but also to products that are costly and unnecessary. And then there's the polite but patronizing way bankers can treat people asking for "firsts"—first car loan, first mortgage, first line of credit and such. In this chapter, you will be equipped to take on banks as your equal.

RECOGNIZE YOUR POTENTIAL

Sure, you have student loans to pay off when you're in your early to mid-twenties and you probably don't have the best-paying job ever. But you are still a valuable client to a bank because of your potential both to improve your earning power as you get older and to increase your demand for products the bank sells. You may see yourself as walking into a bank branch to set up a chequing account. The bank in turn sees a future customer for a mortgage, a line of credit, a credit card, loans, a safe deposit box, financial or investment advice, mutual funds, registered retirement savings plans, guaranteed investment certificates, insurance and more.

The point here is that banks are not doing you a favour in dealing with you—it's the other way around. Bear this in mind if you feel as if you are being treated like a child by bankers.

MEET THE BANKS

Canada's banking system is dominated by the Big Six banks, which is the term used to describe Bank of Montreal, Bank of Nova Scotia, Canadian Imperial Bank of Commerce, National Bank of Canada, Royal Bank of Canada and Toronto-Dominion Bank, which uses the name TD Canada Trust for its branches. There are a few smaller but still substantial banks, like Laurentian Bank, Canadian Western Bank and HSBC Canada, and then there are online banks like President's Choice Financial and ING Direct. As well, there are dozens of credit unions and a few trust companies.

In my experience, here's how they all compare: The big banks offer the lowest interest rates on savings products and the highest fees on day-to-day banking, but they also have the biggest networks of automated teller machines. Considering that it can cost anything from $1.50 to $3 to use another bank's ATMs, this is no small benefit. Online banks—you'll read more about them in this chapter— are great for people who are comfortable with e-commerce, because of the ultra-low fees. Credit unions will often, but not always, give you a break on fees, but their biggest benefit is a more human touch when you deal with their branch staff.

Frankly, friendly staff is one of the lamer reasons to choose a financial institution. With online banking as convenient and easy as it is, you won't be in the branch often enough for it to make a difference. Not too long ago, an executive at one of the big banks presented the idea to me that in an increasingly impersonal, online world, the human touch in a bank branch could make a comeback. I doubt it. I just can't see today's Internet-empowered young adults lining up to see a teller so they can perform a transaction that can be done quickly and easily at an ATM or online at any time of day or night.

Now, which bank are you going to choose? A lot of young adults have accounts at the bank near where they grew up, or where they had their first job. It's all very heartwarming that those ties are being kept, but they may not make business sense. So be open to the idea of switching to a different bank. If you switch, do it when you're a student or new to the workforce, and not later on, when the process can be complicated by pre-arranged automatic deposits into your account and debits from your account. Transferring these transactions to a new account at a different bank is certainly doable, but it's a hassle. A perfect time to make a switch in banks is when you're about to start a full-time job and need to provide your HR department with an account into which your paycheque will be electronically deposited.

STUDENT BANKING

While in college or university, you're eligible for the student banking packages that all the banks offer. As I was writing this, Bank of Montreal offered its Plus Plan to students with the usual $8.50 per month fee waived. Included were up to thirty transactions of all types, one Interac e-Transfer (more on these modern-day replacements for cheques later on in this chapter) and unlimited in-branch bill payments.

Over at Canadian Imperial Bank of Commerce, the CIBC Advantage for Students offered unlimited withdrawals, debits and cheques at no cost. Royal Bank of Canada had the RBC Student Banking package, which provided twenty-five debits per month at no cost, while TD Canada Trust waived the $8.95 charge for the Value Plus Account, with twenty-five transactions per month included. Bank of Nova Scotia took a slightly different approach, charging $1.25 per month for the Student Banking Advantage Plan, which offered unlimited transactions. Banks change their account packages fairly often, so be sure to check for the latest details.

Evaluate your banking needs before picking a student account. Start by figuring out what kind of banking you do. I'm close to 50 years old and I visit a bank branch maybe once or twice a year. I figure that teens and twenty-somethings have to be even more comfortable in the online world, which means they'll value a banking service package that includes the maximum number of debit purchases, bank machine withdrawals and online bill payments. Teller services? Even your parents probably don't use them much. Maybe your grandparents.

The point of finding the right banking package is to minimize service fees. These fees are how banks generate a good part of their impressive profits, and they can apply even to those supposedly free student accounts. Some of those student packages I just mentioned offer a limited number of free transactions. After you've used them up, you start paying for each withdrawal, debit purchase and so forth. Expect to pay fifty to sixty-five cents per transaction once you've used up your freebies. Just ten over the limit will cost you $5, minimum. At the end of the month, the $5 is deducted from your account—in other words, your $5 is now your bank's $5.

Oh, by the way, banks *do* check to make sure you're actually a student. One bank's policy: "Annual proof of full-time registration in a post-secondary university or college or registered vocational school due by Nov. 1st of each year you're enrolled." Essentially, you have to go in once a year and flash some proof of enrolment.

THE WONDERS OF NO-FEE CHEQUING ACCOUNTS

No-fee chequing accounts are available, and they make perfect sense for students and everyone else who is comfortable doing all their banking online. Skeptical about dealing with an online bank? I did it for about a decade, through the now-defunct Citizens Bank of Canada, and had but one complaint. When my bank client card was compromised—it happened at least four or five times over the years—I had to wait for the bank to mail me a new card and username/password (they're sent separately). The process usually took upward of five to seven days, which was a hassle because you need a client card to withdraw cash from a bank machine and pay for things on debit. As a backstop, I kept a plain no-fee savings account at a big bank that had virtually no features other than allowing me to access money in a pinch. Paying for things with a credit card is another alternative if you can't use your bank client card for debits and bank machine withdrawals.

As this was written, no-fee chequing accounts were offered by B.C.'s Coast Capital Savings Credit Union, as well as two online banks, President's Choice Financial and ING Direct. PC Financial is run by the Canadian Imperial Bank of Commerce and the Loblaw's supermarket chain, while ING is the Canadian arm of a huge multinational bank based in the Netherlands. Here's a quick comparison of the no-fee chequing accounts offered by ING and PC Financial:

ING's Thrive Account
- Unlimited free debits and bill payments.
- Fifty free cheques (after that, you pay $12.50 for each order of fifty cheques).
- Free email money transfers.
- So-called Whoops! Protection for up to $250 on over-drawn funds with no fees or interest, provided the money is paid back within thirty days.
- Bank machines in the Exchange network can be used for deposits and withdrawals at no charge (National Bank of Canada, HSBC Bank Canada and many credit unions are part of this network).

PC Financial's No-Fee Bank Account
- Unlimited free debit, bank machine withdrawals (at CIBC ATMs), bill payments and cheques.
- Charge of $4.97 when you go into overdraft (where you write a cheque or make a debit that temporarily leaves your balance below zero), plus interest on the amount you're overdrawn.

- PC points for making various transactions (and you can redeem them for free groceries).
- Bank machines operated by CIBC available at no charge.

The Thrive account was quite new when this book was being written, so there was little feedback available on it. PC Financial has, for the most part, generated extremely positive comments from my readers.

PASS THIS ON TO YOUNGER SIBLINGS

All banks have accounts for little kids. Typically, these involve no fees and pay an inconsequential rate of interest. As a teaching tool, they make sense. As a serious savings account, they're usually a waste of time. One exception comes from ING Direct, which has taken a stab at providing a truly useful account for young kids with its Children's Savings Account. Jointly held by parents and kids, it's a full online savings account complete with a competitive rate of interest. The benefit of having an ING children's account is that a child can, first, earn a decent rate of interest and, second, upgrade to a Thrive no-fee chequing account later on with minimal hassle.

POST-GRADUATION BANKING NEEDS, PART ONE

One of the benefits of having an online no-fee chequing account when you're in school is that you're good to go once you graduate. With the big-bank student accounts, graduation means you'll soon be paying fees for the account you once had at no cost.

If you let your student account slide, your bank will eventually realize that you haven't recently validated your student status and start charging you. As I wrote this, Bank of Montreal claimed to be the only bank offering an extra year of free banking for recent grads.

The best thing to do if you want to deal with a big bank is go onto its website and find an account comparison page. Generally, you'll find four levels of banking packages:

- **Basic:** Costs a few dollars per month; aimed at people who have minimal needs and make only a few withdrawals or debit purchases per month; mainly for hermits.
- **Mid-range:** Costs in the area of $8 or so and offers a few dozen transactions; may work for you if you don't do a lot of withdrawals or use debit a lot.
- **Unlimited:** Costs in the range of $12 per month in exchange for unlimited electronic transactions; charges may apply if you use a teller to, for example, pay a bill.
- **Premium:** For suckers only—fees of $25 or thereabouts and lots of unimportant features.

It's worth noting that many banks will waive your monthly fees if you maintain a set balance—maybe $2,000 or $3,000. That's not easy to do when you're in your early years in the workforce, so never mind. No-fee chequing accounts are a much better deal.

POST-GRADUATION BANKING NEEDS, PART TWO

Everyone needs a chequing account—though not necessarily

to write cheques, as we'll see shortly—and a savings account as well. These two types of accounts are complementary because each does something the other does not.

Chequing accounts are transactional accounts, which is to say they're for the money you will spend until you next get paid. Some chequing accounts pay small amounts of interest, but it's not enough to bother thinking about. That's okay because money in a chequing account is just passing through on the way to covering your day-to-day expenses.

Savings accounts are where you accumulate money you want to keep safe and separate. With your money just sitting there, it makes sense to earn as much interest as you can. Doing this is a challenge because the big banks pay rates that are totally second-rate. Why? They know their clientele includes lots of passive, unsavvy savers who won't take the trouble to find better rates, or who think the bank "brand" is worth something.

I say bank brands are just marketing fluff. Virtually all bank savings deposits are protected for up to $100,000 in value by a federal government–backed agency called the Canada Deposit Insurance Corporation. Whether you're dealing with Royal Bank of Canada or Dutch-owned ING Direct, you have the same level of assurance that your deposits are safe should the bank go under. As this was written, Royal Bank was offering 1.25 per cent on its high-rate savings account, while ING was offering 1.50 per cent.

You could have bumped that up to 2 per cent using Ally, the Canadian arm of a U.S. bank by the same name, or even 2.2 per cent using AcceleRate Financial, an online bank run by the Manitoba-based Crosstown Civic Credit Union. Don't hesitate to go for the bank with the highest rates for savings accounts as long as you can tick off each of these points in the affirmative:

- It's a member of a deposit insurance plan, whether it's CDIC for banks or a provincial plan for credit unions. (I have yet to come across a bank, trust company or credit union that didn't offer accounts protected by deposit insurance.)
- It's convenient to deal with; for online banks, you ideally want to be able to set up electronic transfers between your chequing account at one bank and your savings account elsewhere (you do this by sending a void cheque to the financial institution where your savings account is).
- It offers comparatively high rates for savings on a regular basis, not through a temporary marketing campaign designed to attract new customers; one way to check this is to look on a bank's website for a history of the rates it offers.

THE END OF CHEQUES?

Cheques are a generational thing. For baby boomers, they're a time-tested, zero-worry method of transferring money from one person to another. For younger people, they're the financial equivalent of audio cassette tapes: quite useful in their day, but totally outclassed by modern technology. In the banking biz, modern technology has brought us the e-transfer, which allows people to send money from their bank account to other people via a computer or mobile device. Interac e-Transfer is an example of this service, as are the email money transfers offered through ING Direct's Thrive no-fee chequing account.

With Interac e-Transfer, you need the email address or cell phone number of the recipient, who must have an account with a participating Canadian bank. To ensure that only the recipient can access the money being transferred, you must include a security question that only he or she would be able to answer (favourite movie, name of first dog, father's middle name, middle name of father's first dog, etc.).

Cheques have been with us for roughly three hundred years, and while usage has declined a lot in recent years, they're still going strong. With almost all monthly banking packages, you never pay extra to write or cash a cheque (although you may have to pay for a chequebook). E-transfers, on the other hand, can cost you $1 to $1.50 a crack unless you have one or two free ones included in your bank account package, or you have an account like ING's Thrive, which promotes e-transfers over cheques by offering them for free.

Write cheques if you have to save on fees, but remember that e-transfers offer a newer, often better alternative.

HOTLIST:
TOP BANKING BLUNDERS TO AVOID

- **Racking up excessive ATM fees.** Believe it or not, it wasn't that long ago that you could dip your bank card into any bank's automated teller machine and make a no-fee withdrawal. Today, you can pay upward of $1.50 on the spot to use another bank's ATM, and quite possibly another $1.50 network access fee from your own bank later on. Avoid the no-name ATMs that you see in stores, sports arenas, etc.—they always charge you for access.

- **Paying bills in the branch.** Pay bills online and it's a free transaction with most bank account packages; venture into a branch to have a teller handle the transaction for you and you might pay $1.50 for the service.
- **Last-minute bill payments.** Online banking seems instant, but money you move around using your bank's website may take twenty-four to forty-eight hours to get where it's going. So if your credit card due date is November 15, don't pay it on the fourteenth. Also, the weekend is a dead spot for money being moved electronically. If you pay a bill on Saturday morning, your bank doesn't start processing it until Monday.
- **Careless bill payments.** A misplaced decimal point can be costly when paying bills online, so carefully review each payment before submitting it. Check the date as well, and ensure your account number is correct. Note: You should be able to have a bill payment containing an error called back if you contact your bank immediately by phone.
- **Not reading bank statements.** If you believe banks are infallible, then there's no need to read the monthly account statements. My experience is that errors do happen, and that they're usually fixable if you bring them to your bank's attention. It's a virtual certainty your bank will never come to you to admit an error, unless it involves

money being mistakenly deposited in your account. Note: Banks are increasingly offering account statements online, which is a great option not only because it saves paper but also because the statements are archived online and thus easy to store and refer back to when necessary. Be especially vigilant with bank accounts you don't use a lot. I've heard of cases where fees have mounted up for months on end before the accountholder noticed and put a stop to them. Checking your account often online is another way of making sure everything's okay.

- **Being careless with your bank card PIN.** You are virtually bulletproof against theft or fraud involving unauthorized use of your bank card, provided you have taken reasonable precautions to keep your username and personal identification number private. Don't disclose these passwords to anyone, and never write them down anywhere where a thief who has stolen your bank card might come across them (like on a slip of paper in your wallet or, worse, on the back of the bank card itself). Your bank will have zero sympathy for you if your account gets cleaned out and there's reason to believe you were lax with password security.

- **Being careless about online banking on shared computers.** Bank websites use 128-bit encryption, which makes it highly unlikely that anyone is going to intercept your personal information while you're banking online. But there's an additional security risk of leaving personal information on the computer after you're finished your banking session. If it's your home computer, you should be okay. But if it's a computer at work or in an Internet café, then it's conceivable that someone could end up seeing some of your personal information. Avoid shared computers for online banking, or if you must use one, clear the browser's cache memory, cookies and history when you're done. And of course, make sure no one is looking over your shoulder when you type in your username and password.

- **Getting sucked in by premium bank account packages.** Premium bank accounts can cost as much as $20 to $25 per month, and they're never worth it despite the perks thrown in. Watch out for the bank sales pitch—it usually involves flattering descriptions of you as a serious player who needs a higher level of banking services.

- **Expecting the bank to tell you about its best deals.** It's not unheard of for a banker to suggest a better, cheaper way of doing things, but plan to look after yourself when it comes to getting the best deals on banking. If you're ringing up lots of fees and paying lots of interest, that's revenue for the bank.

- **Neglecting to use your last resort in a dispute with a bank.** All banks have their own internal ombudsman, a person who investigates customer complaints that haven't been resolved by front-line bank staff. If you still can't get any satisfaction and truly believe you're in the right, then escalate your complaint to the Ombudsman for Banking Services and Investments (OBSI) at www.obsi.ca.

- **Getting phished.** Phishing is the process whereby online fraudsters try to fool people into logging into a fake version of an online banking website, thereby disclosing their username and password. This is usually accomplished through what can be amazingly realistic-looking emails apparently sent by a bank's security department. The email asks you to log into your account—when you do, your private information is no longer private. No bank will ever send you an email telling you to log into your account. Ever. Ergo, all emails from banks about security matters are dangerous fakes.

CHAPTER THREE SUMMARY

1. **Take advantage of student banking packages.** They often cost nothing because they're a kind of loss leader for banks.
2. **Squeeze banking fees as low as possible once you're in the workforce.** Look for the lowest-cost chequing account and give strong consideration to online banks with no-fee accounts.
3. **Pay attention to your day-to-day finances.** This helps you stay in control of your spending, helps you cut down on fees and can alert you to fraud in your account.

FOUR

SAVING, BUDGETING AND WHAT TO DO
IF YOU HAVE TO MOVE BACK HOME

Let's start with saving. Given the spotty record of Canadians in this area, it's worth beginning this chapter with a definition. Saving is putting money away today for use later on. When you were a kid, you "saved up" for stuff you would have liked to buy immediately but couldn't afford. As an adult, saving is all that and more. There is short-term saving, for vacations, electronic gadgets and such; medium-term saving, for large expenditures like cars and houses; and long-term saving, for retirement. If all of this sounds unmanageable, get over it. As you make your way through this chapter, you'll learn how to balance savings with all your other financial wants and needs. It's possible, and more important, it's essential. The less skilled you are at saving, the less independent you are. Sure, you can accumulate a lot of junk without saving. That's what credit cards can do for you. But the freedom to choose a nice place to live, drive a decent car, take memorable trips and retire comfortably all depend on your ability as a saver.

POST-GRADUATION FINANCIAL PRIORITIES

There are two priorities to juggle once you finish your university or college education: paying down student loans and building up your savings. Let's define the term "saving" here. It means building up an emergency fund, contingency fund or any other name you care to put on money that's safe and readily accessible for unexpected expenses or emergencies. Once you've got some savings in hand, you can move on to investing for retirement and other priorities.

College and university graduates will get the best bang for their buck by paying off student debt. As we learned in Chapter One, money is lent to students at a rate of prime plus 2.5 per cent for floating-rate loans and prime plus 5 per cent for fixed-rate loans. The prime rate as this book was being written was 3 per cent, which meant people were paying interest on student loans at either 5.5 or 8 per cent. At the same time, the best available rate on a high-rate savings account was 2.2 per cent. In other words, there was an advantage of either 3.3 or 5.8 percentage points for debt repayment over a guaranteed savings return, depending· on which type of loan was involved.

The benefits of paying down debt are less dramatic when compared against the returns you can expect when investing in stocks and bonds as opposed to keeping money in a savings account. Over the long term, you can reasonably expect to make 5 to 7 per cent from a diversified portfolio of stocks and bonds, depending on how much risk you take on. Again, though, you'll want to build up your savings before you get into investing.

Debt repayment looks like a clear winner over saving, which raises the question of whether you should plow all your money into getting rid of your student loans. That's one way to go. Another is to make repaying your debt a priority, while setting a secondary priority of building up your savings/investments. Remember, government loan agencies will dictate your loan repayment schedule. Ideally, you'll be able to keep up with that and have some money left over. Take some of this extra money and pay it down against the balance owing on your loan. Take the rest and put it in a high-rate savings account to start building your emergency fund. How much goes where? A 50–50 split seems a good thought here.

The non-ideal scenario is that you have only enough income to keep current with your student loans. That's okay—you'll still do fine in the long run by retiring your student debt in an orderly way and then moving into savings mode. And remember, help is available if you're unemployed or underemployed and can't keep up with the loan repayment schedule set up for you.

AN INTRODUCTION TO BUDGETING

Post-secondary students should already know something about budgeting. They may or may not have been good at it, but they certainly recognize the imperative of controlling spending so it stays in line with whatever level of income they have. Budgeting as a working adult is more intense, though.

First off, there's the matter of rent. Fall behind and your worst-case scenario involves being kicked out of where you live. Second, you'll have utility bills to pay. Ignore your phone bill and your service will eventually be cut off. Same with hydro and cable. Utility providers will cut you some slack, but it's limited.

Budgeting is how you ensure money is available to meet your debts and savings goals, and have some left over to enjoy life. It's not so important how much you make. What matters is that you take control.

BUDGETING BASICS

- **Prioritize.** Pay the rent first, because you don't want to get kicked out of your apartment. Actually, it's human nature to put rent or mortgage payments first. That's why banks let people take on big mortgage payments— they know borrowers will put mortgage payments ahead of their other debts. Regular monthly expenses like hydro and heat are another priority, and so is repayment of student loans, if applicable.
- **Visualize.** When planning your life, from grocery shopping to social activities, keep in mind how much cash you have to play with. One of the cruel lessons of budgeting is that if you overspend this week, you'll almost certainly overspend in the following weeks and dig an ever-larger deficit (facilitated by credit cards, usually).

- **The emergency fund.** Some experts say you should have enough secure cash on hand to pay three months' worth of expenses. Sure, and you should have eight servings of veggies and fruit per day, avoid alcohol and always think pure thoughts. There are the ideals of personal finance, and there are the realities. Simply having "some" cash on hand for emergencies is much better than nothing. Start with a couple of hundred dollars in a high-interest savings account and try to build up to a few thousand dollars.

A SAMPLE BUDGET

Here's a rough list of some of things that, on a weekly or monthly basis, will use up the take-home pay of someone who is renting an apartment:

- Food (groceries, lunches, coffee, restaurant meals)
- Transportation (public transit tickets or passes, gas and car maintenance)
- Utilities (phone, hydro, cable TV, Internet)
- Cell phone
- Entertainment

Here are some big annual or monthly expenses to budget for as well:

- Rent
- Student loan repayment
- Renters insurance
- Car insurance

Here are some potential emergencies or surprise expenses that can crop up and cost you serious money:

- Car breakdown
- Major dental work that isn't covered by an employer group plan
- Income tax owing

LET TECHNOLOGY DO YOUR BUDGETING FOR YOU

Budgeting is one of the most tedious activities known to humankind. It's like counting the grains in a package of rice—you think you have a handle on things, and then you lose count or find something you missed. So let's look at alternatives to traditional budgeting, where you tally up all your various expenses and then compare them to your income. Instead, we'll look at using the capabilities of online banking to control your day-to-day spending so that everything gets taken care of automatically.

Most banks, including both PC Financial and ING Direct, offer high-interest, no-fee savings accounts that work well as a complement to their chequing accounts. You'll want to open at least two or three of these savings accounts for your auto-budgeting system.

Once all your accounts are up and running online, you'll set up a series of ongoing automatic transfers of cash from your chequing account to your savings accounts. Arrange to have the transfers made on the day your paycheque is deposited into your chequing account. Saving for a trip or a car? Decide how much you want to put away each pay period and then arrange for that amount to be automatically transferred into one of your savings accounts (some banks allow you to nickname your accounts, along the lines of "Car Savings" or "Trip Account").

Worried about having enough cash in your account to cover your monthly rent cheque? Then arrange to have a fraction of your rent deposited into one of your savings accounts every time you get paid. Then when you write your rent cheque, transfer the full rental amount from savings to chequing.

You can also use the automatic transfer method to save bit by bit to cover large annual expenditures like car insurance or a health club membership. Whatever your expenditure or savings goal, you can ensure you're on track by setting up automatic transfers into a dedicated savings account.

For a more traditional approach to budgeting combined with modern technology, check out a very cool website called Mint.com. Popular for years in the United States, Mint came to Canada in late 2010. It's a free online service that allows you to track your spending day by day and compare it to pre-set guidelines you create for yourself. You might say that $100 a week is your limit for restaurant meals, movies and DVDs. Mint will tell you whether you're meeting this goal, and if not, by how much you're missing. By giving Mint the passwords to all your bank and investment accounts, you can also get a big-picture view of your net worth. Worried about security? Mint uses heavy-duty encryption and allows only its computer network to handle your private data (that means no people). Note: The federal Financial Consumer Agency of Canada has issued a warning that disclosing user IDs and passwords to third-party aggregators (that's what Mint is) means you're breaking your cardholder agreement and thereby voiding any security guarantees you have. The FCAC said that its warning was issued to make people aware of the possible ramifications of sharing user IDs and passwords, and that there were no reported incidents of fraud related to aggregators like Mint.

ONLINE BUDGETING HELP

The FCAC offers a very useful online budgeting calculator that works for people of all generations, including students and recent graduates. There's a slot to add income from student loans, and another to add student loan repayments. Check it out here: www.fcac-acfc.gc.ca/eng/consumers/itools/budget/index-eng.asp.

CREDIT VS. DEBIT VS. CASH FOR DAY-TO-DAY SPENDING

Debit is far better than credit from the point of view of smart money management, and cash is better than debit. Credit creates the mirage of buying things without paying. Debit is closer to reality because, while no money changes hands at the store, the cost of a purchase is immediately taken out of your bank account. Cash is concrete. You have it, you spend it and then you don't have it anymore.

Okay, now that we've dispensed with the wholesome Parental Guidance view of credit and cash, let's get adult. You generate by far the most value for your spending when you use your credit card for every possible purchase and then pay off your balance no later than the due date on your statement. When I use my credit card to pay for gas and groceries, I usually pay what I owe within twenty-four hours, using online banking. Assuming you have a well-chosen reward card, each purchase will generate points of one sort or another (or cash, in the case of cash-back cards). These points represent economic value that is not enjoyed by people paying cash. Note: It's a growing trend for reward cards to provide extra points for grocery, gas and drugstore purchases. Examples:

- **CIBC's Aerogold Visa card:** Gives you 1.5 miles per dollar spent, instead of one point.
- **Bank of Nova Scotia Momentum Visa:** Pays 2 per cent cash back on gas, groceries and drugstore purchases, compared with 1 per cent on other purchases.
- **MBNA Smart Cash Platinum Plus:** A no-fee card (unlike the two previous cards) that pays 3 to 5 per cent cash back on qualifying gas and grocery purchases.

Don't even think about using your credit card this way unless you have the iron discipline necessary to keep your weekly spending in line and get your card bill paid off each month in full. It's one thing to pay off sporadic credit card purchases like a dinner out or some clothes. It's a much bigger challenge to pay off all that, plus four weeks' worth of groceries, gasoline, lunches and such.

HOTLIST:
FIVE ROOKIE FINANCIAL MISTAKES TO AVOID

- **Bouncing cheques.** Writing cheques for sums you don't have sitting in your bank account can hurt you in a few ways. First, your bank can slap you with a NSF (non-sufficient funds) fee of up to $40 or so. Second, the recipient of the cheque will think you're a fool, or worse. Third, it can damage your credit rating.
- **Not having overdraft protection on your bank account.** Overdraft protection, which is basically insurance against temporarily using up more money than you have in your account, is a must-have unless you are meticulous about ensuring you have enough money to cover all your needs. Some banks charge you a little bit each month for overdraft, while others offer this feature at no cost. All will charge daily interest at a hefty rate on your overdrawn balance. Better to pay these costs than to bounce a cheque or miss an automated monthly bill payment.
- **Not paying attention to whether you have the right bank account package.** If you want to get all scientific about this, you can check the account offerings of various banks online and find the one that sounds best for you (start with the ING Direct and PC Financial accounts mentioned earlier in this chapter). Or if you're happy with your existing bank, check its website or consult an account rep in a branch to see if you've got the most cost-effective account. The rule to follow: you want the most electronic transactions (i.e., debits and bank machine

withdrawals) for the least amount of money per month. In-branch service is for seniors.

- **Staying loyal to one bank.** Be financially promiscuous. For each of your banking needs, look for the best deal. No bank is at the cutting edge in every product area.

- **Not understanding what the banking business is all about.** Very quickly, it's about selling products and making money for the bank. Banks will put their interests ahead of yours, all the more so if you're a rookie who accepts at face value what you're told by your banker. Make your dealings with the bank a dialogue where you ask plenty of questions. Note the answers, and if they sound self-serving or unclear, do some further research online. Google your questions, check other bank websites or email me at rcarrick@globeandmail.com. There's hardly anything a bank can tell you that I haven't heard before.

WHEN PLANS GO AWRY: INTRODUCING THE BOOMERANG GENERATION

We've been talking here as if you have made a successful transition from school to the workforce, with a decent salary, a place to live and the upward mobility we all expect at this time of life. It may not happen, though. A tight economy can make it tough to find a job. Or maybe you haven't found the necessary focus to land gainful employment (you've been slacking, in other words).

Let me tell you a story about my early post-university days. I thought I had a job lined up for at least the summer following graduation, but I learned just before school ended that it had fallen through. I moved back home. I applied for many jobs, got some interviews and was offered a few things that I turned down. All the while, my parents were supportive without being patsies. On the whole, I think they were happy to have me back at home after being away at school.

Aside from a little freelancing here and there (I wrote something for a sporting goods magazine on the latest in ski equipment, even though I had never been on skis in my life), I was unemployed from April through the summer and into the fall. Then, after checking in with the employer I thought I had a job with before graduation, I was offered a temporary position. I took it, moving out within a few weeks, and my life as a working adult began.

My point here is that a little parental support at a key moment can help position you for a lifetime of success. If it happens that you need to move back home, you can at least tell your parents you're not unique. In fact, there are enough young adults in this position that a catchphrase has emerged to describe them—the Boomerang Generation. Boomerang kids left home, stayed away for a while and now are back.

The boomerang phenomenon gained notice during the recession that ended the last decade. Better economic times may put this catchphrase to rest, but that doesn't mean parents won't have to make boomerang decisions like:

- **Whether they should charge you room and board.** This is totally discretionary on their part. If they feel you're a responsible, financially savvy, ambitious kid who has hit a patch of bad luck, then maybe they won't see any need to charge you room and board. If they think you could benefit from the structure of paying for accommodations, they may decide to arrange a monthly payment. Still another possibility is that you move back home to save money for the purchase of a house or some other savings goal. Here, it's totally a judgment call about whether to charge you for accommodation.

- **Whether to provide some day-to-day spending cash.** Personally, I wouldn't mind spotting my hard-up kid a bit of money here and there to enjoy a social life. Providing, of course, that he or she was working overtime to find a decent job.
- **Whether to push you to take any job you can get.** A career-minded graduate with decent credentials and a focused job-search approach should not be encouraged to take anything that pays a salary. We're talking about career-building here, not casual or part-time work. The day may come, though, when your parents have to say it's time to find some gainful employment of any type.

I BELONG TO THE BOOMERANG GENERATION (AND I CAN TAKE IT OR LEAVE IT EACH TIME)

Apologies for appropriating Richard Hell's nihilistically poetic song "Blank Generation," but it seemed relevant to the much newer Boomerang Generation. Media coverage of this demographic seems to tilt toward the perspective of the unfortunate parent, as in the young 'uns have left home to go to college or university and it's not natural for them to come back. Well, no kidding. Very few twentysomethings *want* to move back home after a period away at school. Back to your little room, with your little bed and the big-boy desk your parents bought you when you were five. Back to your parents knowing when you leave and when you get home (and with whom). Back to sharing bathrooms with siblings and doing household chores you thought you were off the hook for until you bought your own home.

HOTLIST:
HOW TO HANDLE THE 'RENTS IF YOU HAVE TO MOVE BACK HOME

As undesirable as it might be for you to move back home, it's a very real possibility in today's highly competitive and specialized job market. Here are some suggestions on how to handle the financial aspects of moving back with your parents:

- **Be an adult.** Rather than just announcing your imminent return engagement *chez parents*, tell your mom and dad that you are having cashflow difficulties and would like to discuss the idea of moving back home for a while.
- **Have a plan.** Tell your parents what you plan to do to find work, and how long you estimate it may take. Make it clear you're building a career, not looking for hours at Tim Hortons.
- **Offer to pay.** Figure out how much you can reasonably afford to pay for your room and board and make the offer. Best case, they tell you, "Thanks for offering, but that's not necessary."

- **Contribute in a non-financial way.** Shovelling snow, cutting grass, doing dishes and taking out the garbage are ways to offset the extra costs your parents are incurring (like groceries, for one thing).
- **Contribute in a financial way.** Buy the groceries one week, send your parents out to dinner, buy them Leafs TV for a year.
- **Keep them updated.** Get out in front of all the questions your parents are inevitably going to have about what you're doing to find work and how things are going. Understand that they're not trying to hassle you; rather, they're concerned and want to see you moving on to the next steps in life.
- **Accept advice.** Hey, your parents have probably been in the workforce for a few decades. They may have some legit ideas about finding a job.

TOUGHER ECONOMIC TIMES?

Back in late 2010, *Maclean's* magazine ran a cover story with the headline "Generation Screwed: Lower Incomes. Worse Jobs. Higher Taxes. Bleaker Futures. What Boomers Are Leaving Their Children." I think *Maclean's* was on to something. First, though, let's acknowledge that people were still feeling the after-effects of a global financial crisis and recession at the time that piece appeared. Pessimism was trendy; optimism was scarce.

But even if you discount for passing gloom, there are still trends at work that will make it harder for today's young adults to enjoy the same economic success as their parents. For one thing, older workers are staying in the workforce longer. Statistics Canada has reported that between October 2009 and October 2010, the fastest rate of employment growth was among workers aged 55 and over. At the same time, there was an offsetting decline in employment for those aged 25 to 54.

Another factor is the alarming state of government finances. As politically toxic as tax increases are, it's hard to see all levels of government balancing their budgets without raising taxes. Cuts in government services are likely as well, regardless of whether taxes rise. Translation: you'll quite possibly have to pay more for things like a university or college education and health care.

I raise this discouraging outlook for one simple reason—as context for discussions parents and their young adult children will have as they consider the issues covered in this chapter. The Boomerang Generation: defined by necessity, not by choice.

CHAPTER FOUR SUMMARY

1. **Debt repayment is crucial.** Clearing away debts built up as a student is the first step toward good financial health as an adult.

2. **Learn about budgeting.** You may not live day to day using a budget, but a comparison of your expected costs against your income is a useful way to see how much room you have to pay off debt and save.

3. **Be aware of the boomerang effect.** Economic necessity may send twentysomethings back to the family home for a

while. If it happens to you, offer to help out your parents with money or help around the house—don't be a sponge.

CASE STUDY: Sarah

Sarah, 26, studied sociology and anthropology at an East Coast university and then returned to her hometown of Ottawa to take a two-year community college program in gerontology. After graduation, she found part-time work as an activity assistant in a retirement home. Sarah lived both in residence and off campus while attending university, and she returned to live at home for the next phase of her education. She continues to live at home while working because her salary isn't enough to cover rent on an apartment, but she has made considerable headway paying off her student loans.

Graduated when? Eight months earlier.

Annual employment income: $19,500.

Estimated total education costs: $57,000.

Primary source of money to cover tuition and other educational expenses: RESP, student line of credit.

Amount of student loans: $25,000.

Started repaying student loans? Yes.

Total amount of student loans still outstanding? $5,500.

Where are you living, post-graduation? At home.

What was behind your decision to return home? I couldn't afford to rent an apartment.

Are you paying rent at home? Yes, $200 a month.

Is living at home comfortable or just a stopgap? It's comfortable for now, but I am looking forward to having my own place.

What's your biggest financial mistake since graduating? I'm actually fairly frugal, especially when it comes to purchasing things for myself. While I was taking college courses in the evenings, I would work, and the money I earned would go toward paying for classes.

What's your smartest financial move since graduating? Buying a car (it helped my credit rating). I invested some of my savings into GICs, which earn interest and allow me some breathing room.

What have been your biggest financial stresses when starting in the workforce? Figuring out how much to save, how much to invest, what I can afford to live on. With all those stories of the younger generation not putting anything aside in RRSPs, I'm feeling pressure to not only pay down my student debt but also start saving for my retirement. With another thirty-five years of working ahead of me, it all feels rather daunting.

Best advice on affording college or university for other young adults? Take one or two summer courses each year; then during the regular school year, take four courses instead of five. One reason is that there's more time for a part-time job to help pay for any expenses. Another reason is that courses during the summer tend to be cheaper, and the cost for any books needed isn't as overwhelming as when you have to buy ten textbooks at once.

Any advice you wish you'd received? To think about what a degree is worth. After my B.A., I still had two more years in college ahead of me to earn the practical certification program I needed in order to get any work in my field.

Are you managing to save any money? Yes. I have a system for dividing up my paycheque. I put a little on my line of credit and my auto insurance and then some in savings, and whatever is leftover I use to pay for my phone, gas and other expenses.

FIVE

LOOKING TO THE FUTURE: RRSPs AND TFSAs

In Canada, we expect people to take an adult attitude toward saving for retirement. True, we have the Canada Pension Plan, which you will almost certainly be enrolled in if you're over the age of 18 and earn a salary. But the CPP and other government programs aren't enough to generate the income that most people will need in retirement. To cover that gap, you have to save for yourself. You have to take a disciplined, long-term approach that involves steady contributions made over decades. You have to maintain your retirement savings approach even while juggling the costs of buying a home, having kids, travelling and buying stuff. In other words, you have to be an adult about retirement saving.

It sucks, I know. The last thing you'll want to do in your early years in the workforce is put money away so you can use it forty or fifty years down the road. Do it anyway. A moderate, steady approach to retirement saving is the best present you can give your future self. I don't buy into the never-ending drama in this country about how people simply aren't saving enough for retirement. In large part, that's financial industry propaganda designed to sell mutual funds. But if we're going to take an adult attitude toward retirement saving, it means no procrastination, no avoiding of responsibility and no feigning ignorance. If you accept that, then you'll realize that the time to start saving for life as a senior is in your twenties or early thirties.

WHAT YOUR PARENTS CAN CONTRIBUTE

Not money, but the benefit of their experience. One of the best pieces of financial advice my own father gave me was to start a registered retirement savings plan while I was in my mid-twenties. I had recently started working full time and he put the idea in my head at a time when I was thinking about cars, trips and other forms of immediate gratification. RRSPs were as much of a concern to me then as the weather on Mars. Still, I took my dad's advice and opened an RRSP at my bank. I can't say how much that money's worth today, but I can say I got an early introduction to retirement saving that gave me decades of time to work with.

A perfect way to frame the conversation is to ask your parents about the state of their retirement savings. If they're right on track—maybe they have a solid pension or substantial savings in RRSPs—get them to explain how they got there. If they're not confident about their level of savings, let this be a lesson to you on the benefit of getting an early start on saving for retirement.

ORDER OF OPERATIONS: WHAT TO DO FIRST

Here's a game plan for a recent graduate who has just entered the workforce: pay off your student debt and any credit card debt you may have incurred while in school, build up your savings and then get around to investing for retirement. A gradual move into retirement saving is certainly viable after your debts are under control and you have some money in a savings account. No one expects you to lead a monastic life of austerity where you sacrifice to pay off student debt, build up a plush emergency fund and then immediately switch over to all-out retirement saving. You are entitled to enjoy your new freedom as a salaried adult. As long as you can afford it without building up debt (especially credit card debt), buy yourself some stuff. Buy some furniture for your apartment or the latest i-whatever gadget. Take a trip. Eat and drink well. Don't neglect retirement saving, but keep it on simmer for a very short while. Later—but not much later—you can dial it up to a boil.

RRSPs FOR TWENTYSOMETHINGS: ONE EXPERT'S PERSPECTIVE

One recent RRSP season, a big bank issued a news release quoting poll results indicating that the number of young adults aged 18 to 34 with RRSPs had fallen close to the lowest level in a decade, at 39 per cent. Moreover, 45 per cent of people in this age group had not started saving for retirement, and overall, retirement saving ranked seventh on a list of financial priorities, behind debt repayment, saving for a rainy day and home ownership.

In summarizing the findings of its poll, the bank hinted that young adults were missing out on the benefits of RRSPs, which not uncoincidentally are a major source of revenue for banks and other financial firms. To find out whether young adults were on the wrong track, I consulted one of the country's most independent thinkers on retirement matters, actuary Malcolm Hamilton of the pension consulting firm Mercer. Here's an edited transcript of our conversation:

Young adults seem to be shirking on RRSPs—do these results alarm you?
No. Debt reduction probably should be a priority, as should buying a home, if you're going to buy one.

Are young adults doomed to poverty in their senior years if they don't start saving for retirement right away?
When you look at people that age, they're just starting out. It's impossible to look at what they're doing and say their life is going to be a financial catastrophe. There are countless decisions they need to make over the next few years that will ultimately determine whether they've behaved sensibly and prudently or not.

Do you have any concerns about how well today's young adults will make out in retirement?
The baby boomers typically got married in their twenties,

had children in their late twenties or early thirties and amortized their mortgages over twenty-five years. [Amortization is the time horizon for paying off a mortgage in full.] They had their financial burdens behind them or reduced by their mid-forties or early fifties. Today, people are graduating later and carrying more [student] debt; they marry later, have kids later, buy homes later; and they amortize mortgages over longer periods. For this generation, [the debt-free years] may not happen until they're 55 or 60.

Does this mean they may have to retire later than their parents to top up their savings?
The good news is that they'll live longer and be able to work longer.

What's the best financial advice for young adults?
Live reasonably frugally and don't waste money.

THE ABCs OF RRSPs

The primary vehicle for retirement savings is the registered retirement savings plan, which is not itself an investment product. RRSP is a term to describe an investment account holding mutual funds, term deposits, stocks, bonds or other investments that is registered with the Canada Revenue Agency and is designed as way to save for retirement. Investment gains in an RRSP are sheltered from taxes, which allows them to compound over the decades and build your retirement savings.

Compounding is an important financial concept—so it's important to understand it correctly. Basically, it refers to the way investment returns in your RRSP team up with the money you yourself contributed to build your savings over the years. If you start with $1,000 in an RRSP and earn a 5 per cent return in a year, you would have $1,050 after one year. If you earn another 5 per cent in the next year, it would apply to your initial $1,000 investment and to last year's $50 investment return. Over decades, the impact of compounding in your RRSP can be tremendous.

Next, let's make sure you understand the tax aspect of RRSPs. When you make a contribution to a plan, it's generally with money on which you've already paid taxes. In completing your annual tax return, you'll note how much you contributed to RRSPs and the government will refund the taxes paid on that amount. RRSPs are not tax-free, though. When you retire, you will pay tax on money withdrawn from your plan.

Misunderstanding the tax refund is one of the most common mistakes people make with RRSPs. This refund is not some sort of bonus designed to reward you for contributing to your own retirement saving. Rather, it's designed to prevent you from being subjected to double taxation. You contribute to an RRSP with after-tax dollars, and then you'll pay tax on RRSP withdrawals when you're retired. Refunding tax on contributions eliminates the first of these tax hits.

By the way, you're supposed to reinvest the tax refund your RRSP generates back into your retirement savings, or else use it to pay down debt or for some other financially worthy cause. Using a little to pay for a vacation or to cover a big expense is okay, too. Ya gotta live a little.

RRSPs are available literally everywhere—from banks and credit unions, insurance agents, financial planners, investment dealers and online brokers. There's no "best" choice when you're young and just starting to put money in an RRSP. The key is simply to get going. Frankly, your whole RRSP strategy when you're in your twenties and early thirties should come down first, to finding good investment products to use—say, mutual funds or exchange-traded funds—and second, to making regular contributions—say, every time you're paid, or every month, through automatic transfer from your chequing account to your investment account.

PARENTAL GUIDANCE ON RRSPs

Put your parents' investing experience to work in helping you start your retirement savings. Ask your parents if they know of some good mutual funds or exchange-traded funds. If they're proficient at investing and handle their own money, consider asking them to help you set up a self-directed RRSP account with an online broker.

If your parents have a smart financial adviser, maybe he or she can take on your RRSP. Your parents would actually be doing their adviser a favour in bringing over your account. Young people certainly start small, but the growth potential is huge. As a recent graduate, you will be investing for decades, building assets in RRSP accounts, RESP accounts, tax-free savings accounts and possibly non-registered investment accounts as well. That's big revenue potential for an adviser.

INVESTING IN RRSPs 101

Smart investing for any purpose starts with deciding on an appropriate mix of stocks, bonds and cash. You can own stocks directly, but mutual funds and exchange-traded funds are preferable for beginners. You can own bonds directly, but mutual funds and ETFs holding bonds are good alternatives, and guaranteed investment certificates are even better. Cash means money that is kept safe and liquid, which means that it's available quickly and not vulnerable to what the financial markets are doing. You can let money sit in cash in your RRSP account (it will probably earn no interest), or you can use a money market fund or a high-interest savings product.

FUND PRIMER: MUTUAL FUNDS AND EXCHANGE-TRADED FUNDS

MUTUAL FUNDS. Owning a mutual fund is essentially like having a share of a pool of stocks and/or bonds selected by a professional money manager for the fund's clients. The cost to buy mutual funds can range from zero to 2 per cent of the amount you're investing, and the cost of owning them typically reduces your returns by 1.5 to 2.5 per cent. Fund companies pay themselves these fees by scooping them off the top of fund returns. When you see a mutual fund's return published somewhere, it virtually always reflects an after-fee amount. **EXCHANGE-TRADED FUNDS (ETFS).** ETFs are usually, but not always, designed to provide the return of major stock and bond indexes, minus a much smaller fee than mutual funds charge. ETFs trade like stocks, which means you need a brokerage account to buy them and you must pay commissions for each transaction. Online brokers will charge you between $5 and $29 to buy and sell ETFs, depending on which firm you choose and how large your account is.

Depending on your age, the money you contribute to an RRSP in your early working years will be invested for many decades before you start using it. So don't be nervous about investing in the stock market. That's easy to say, but apparently not so easy to do. As I wrote this, the after-effects of the market crash of 2008–09 were still fresh enough to scare a wide swath of investors away from the stock market. Surprisingly, young investors were leaders in this trend.

In early 2011, a report on the CNNMoney.com website noted two surveys of young adult Americans that showed a striking trend toward conservative investing. One of the surveys, conducted by an organization of mutual fund companies, found that only 34 per cent of people under age thirty-five were willing to take substantial or above-average risks in their portfolios, down from 48 per cent in 2005. A survey by the U.S. investment dealer Merrill Lynch found that among people 34 and younger, more than half said they had a low tolerance for risk. Strangely, people aged 35 to 64 indicated they had significantly more tolerance for risk, even though their closer proximity to retirement left them less time to make back money lost in the stock market. These are U.S. results, but they certainly are valid here in Canada. It's worth noting that Canadian investors are actually somewhat more cautious than U.S. investors on the whole.

Horrendous stock market slumps like we saw in 2008— and in 2001 and 2002—usually scare people away from stocks for a few years. So maybe the fear of stocks documented in those surveys will slowly fade away. Just in case it doesn't, let's review some facts.

Yes, the stock market can fall hard. In 2008, the year of the great global financial crisis, the Canadian market plunged a shocking 33 per cent. But the next year it made 35 per cent, and the year after that it made 17.6 per cent. By the end of 2010, the average annual return for the Canadian market over the previous twenty years was 9.8 per cent if you include dividends as well as increases in share prices. The point here is that stock market returns can be attractive when you hold for a long period of time, even if there are short-term plunges.

As you get into your later fifties you will want to reduce your exposure to stocks so as to avoid having your RRSP annihilated in a 2008-like market setback. But when you're young, with many decades of investing ahead, it's best to have most of your RRSP investments in the stock market. You can make a case for having your entire RRSP in the stock market in your late twenties and early thirties, but don't do this unless you're the kind of person who doesn't worry about temporary investing setbacks (I bet you're not that kind of a person). A more livable approach would be for a 30-year-old to have 70 to 80 per cent of her RRSP in the stock market and the rest in bonds and cash.

There's no certifiably correct mix of investments at any age—only guidelines. One of the oldest is to subtract your age from 100 and use that number as the percentage of your RRSP that goes into the stock market, with the rest going into bonds. To reflect longer lifespans, some experts now suggest subtracting your age from 110 or even 120 to find your appropriate level of stock market exposure.

Your own temperament is a factor, too. If you just can't stomach having a big portion of your RRSP in the stock market, don't do it. Just recognize that a lower level of risk will mean lower returns over the long term, and this in turn suggests you'll need to contribute more to your retirement savings to achieve the amount needed to fund your retirement. When investing, risk brings you the potential for larger returns (and larger losses), and safety limits you to smaller returns.

A quick word about bonds to close this section. Bonds are a great stabilizer for your RRSP because they tend to do well in periods when the stock markets are falling hard. But here's a reason not to overdo it on bonds: they've performed much better in the past twenty years than we can expect them to in the future. A rising interest rate outlook is a key explanation. From the mid-1990s through 2010, interest rates were on a near-steady path lower. That's an ideal environment for investing in bonds, because a bond rises in value when rates fall (and vice versa). Rates hit rock bottom in the recession of 2008–09 and stayed there as the global economy struggled. Still, the long-term expectation was a multiyear rate rebound that would not be good for bonds.

WHAT ABOUT YOUR PARENTS' RETIREMENT SAVINGS?

Wait a second, aren't we talking here about how twenty- and thirtysomethings can prepare for retirement? Yes, and to be thorough we have to look at all eventualities. One of them is that your parents may not have sufficient retirement savings and thus have to rely on you to help them out in their senior years.

There are a few different ways parents can end up depending on their kids. It could be with some cash to cover a sudden expenditure—maybe a new roof for the house or a major car repair. It could be a loan to tide them over until the sale of the family home is complete. Or the parental assistance could take the form of medical costs—say, twenty-four-hour in-home nursing care.

If they find they are financially struggling after they retire, your parents shouldn't hesitate to ask you for help if they need it. That's what families do for each other. But if your parents value their financial independence, it couldn't hurt for you to check in with them early about how their retirement savings plan is coming along. The good news for your parents is that they probably still have some years to go before they retire, and that means there's at least a little time to address any shortcomings. In fact, the years after their kids move out can be a prime retirement savings period for parents.

Here's a low-stress way to get a conversation going with your parents about their retirement saving. Tell them that you've recently been getting your own RRSP going and you want to exchange ideas. During the conversation, ask your parents how confident they are about a financially comfortable retirement. It's a bad sign if they have no idea of how much they have or will need in retirement, or if they evade the topic as if it's painful to talk about.

If your parents have a financial adviser, they should have a retirement plan in place. Are they sketchy on the details? Then they should schedule a meeting and ask how much they're on track to have saved by retirement, and what kind of lifestyle that amount is likely to finance. If there's a shortfall, they can plan to work longer or contribute more to their RRSPs.

THREE PATHS FOR STARTING AN RRSP

These suggestions are based on the idea that it's more important to get going with an RRSP than it is to pick the perfect way of investing. Most people change their RRSP accounts a few times as they get more experience with financial matters.

Head to Your Bank

All banks and credit unions have staff who can sell you mutual funds.

What to buy: Almost all the banks have good Canadian dividend funds, which invest in big blue-chip companies that pay cash dividends to shareholders each quarter. (Dividends are paid by successful, stable companies that generate more profit than is needed to keep the business running well.) Consider arranging to have 70 or 80 per cent of your contributions go into this dividend fund, and the rest in a Canadian bond fund.

Examples of dividend funds: BMO Dividend, CIBC Dividend Growth, RBC Canadian Dividend, Scotia Canadian Dividend, TD Dividend Growth, Ethical Canadian Dividend (available at credit unions).

Caveat emptor: When you deal with one fund provider, you've got the responsibility of picking through both good and bad funds. No single fund company does everything well.

Open an Online Brokerage Account

Most banks have online brokerage divisions, and branch staff can help you open an account. You can also open an account online. If you're willing to shop around, check out my annual *Globe and Mail* ranking of online brokers at www.theglobeandmail.com/globe-investor/2010-online-broker-rankings/the-12th-annual-online-broker-rankings/article1790577/.

What to buy: Forget about individual stocks until you've something like $50,000 in your account; to build your assets, consider low-cost mutual funds, exchange-traded funds and GICs.

Examples: The Claymore family of ETFs offers a great service whereby you can pay to make an initial investment in one of its funds and then add more money every month or every three months at no cost. A good start would be the Claymore Canadian Fundamental Index ETF (ticker symbol CRQ on the Toronto Stock Exchange), which gives you exposure to the Canadian stock market. You could pair that up with the Claymore 1-5 Year Laddered Government Bond Index Fund (CLF). Also, the online brokerage Scotia iTrade has introduced commission-free trading for some ETFs.

Caveat emptor: Some people get overwhelmed and intimidated when investing for themselves, and that can lead to a state of paralysis, where RRSP money sits idly in cash and never gets invested. You also need to understand enough about investing to build a sound portfolio. Mistakes are made by all investors—the trick is to get the important things right, like a proper mix of exposure to stocks and bonds.

Find a Financial Adviser

Your parents might have one they use and like; you can also ask friends, family and co-workers for recommendations, or check out advisers who have offices near your home or office. Another option is to try a search engine like the following:

- AccretiveAdvisor: www.accretiveadvisor.com/
- Know Your Financial Advisor: kyfa.com/ca
- Financial Planning Standards Council: www.fpsc.ca/ directory-cfp-professionals-good-standing
- Advocis: www.advocis.ca/content/find-ad-form.aspx

Interview an adviser before signing on, and ask questions about what kind of service you will get as a young adult with only a small account, what type of financial planning is offered, whether the adviser deals with other young people and how the adviser charges for her services. Forging a solid relationship with an adviser as a young adult could be the smartest financial move you ever make.

What to buy: Virtually all advisers will offer you mutual funds as a beginner investor.

Examples: Your adviser will choose funds for you, but you can have some say in the process by requesting funds with low fees and by rejecting funds sold with a deferred sales charge (no commissions to purchase, but you pay a redemption fee if you want to sell your holdings in the first several years after you buy). Ask your adviser about zero-load funds. That's where your adviser waives the upfront sales commission on funds and there's no redemption fee. There are also front-load funds, where the adviser charges you 2 or 3 per cent to buy funds (again, no redemption fee).

Caveat emptor: Some advisers are just mutual fund salespeople who don't provide much advice at all. The fees you pay to buy and own mutual funds typically include compensation that is paid by your fund company to your adviser. Make sure this flow of money is earned by your adviser with lots of advice.

THE SMARTEST RRSP SAVINGS STRATEGY OF THEM ALL

This is deceptively simple. Start early with RRSP contributions and then make regular payments year after year. I do this, but I think I'm in the minority, judging by the persistence of a particularly dumb financial ritual called RRSP season.

You'll notice RRSP season getting under way in January, with lots of advertising by banks, mutual fund companies and advice firms. It then runs through February to a deadline somewhere around March 1. That's the last date for making an RRSP contribution that will count toward the previous tax year, and it's always a busy one for banks and advisers. Often, you'll see branches staying open to midnight to accommodate the worst procrastinators.

The financial industry is happy to beef up service for the RRSP deadline because it helps suck in dollars that generate revenue through fees and commissions. Why investors participate in RRSP season, I'll never know. It's not only more time-efficient to get on a regular, automatic RRSP savings program, but also more comfortable from a psychological point of view.

First off, let's define an automatic RRSP savings plan. It involves you arranging to have money electronically transferred from your chequing account into your RRSP account every payday or every month. You could do it quarterly, too, but you'll find the drain on your cash flow much easier to manage if you contribute lesser amounts more frequently. The key to an automatic RRSP plan is that it's nondiscretionary. No matter what financial diversions emerge, you're building your retirement savings on a steady basis.

Don't just contribute the money to your RRSP and let it sit there in cash. Choose some quality mutual funds or ETFs to buy gradually. This is called dollar-cost averaging, which means you'll be buying at both high and low points for the stock markets and your cost will be averaged out. Frankly, some studies have shown that plunking down a big chunk of change can get you a better return for your investment dollars, but psychologically, dollar-cost averaging is the better strategy for the most investors. First, it keeps people buying during bad times for the stock market. That's when you're supposed to buy, but most people don't have the confidence. Dollar-cost averaging also prevents you from jumping into an overheated market, when the upside is almost gone and downside risk looms. Instead, you chug along month by month and year by year, contributing without fail and building your retirement savings assets.

Set the amount of your contributions by figuring out how much you want to add annually to your RRSP and dividing by twelve or twenty-six. When arranging your automatic plan, don't forget to keep your RRSP properly balanced. If you have a portfolio mix of 70 per cent stocks and 30 per cent bonds, break a $100 monthly contribution into $70 for an equity fund and $30 for a bond fund. Once a year, rebalance your holdings by selling your winners and buying your losers so you get back to a 70–30 mix.

LEAKY RRSPs

RRSPs should be considered untouchable, one-way savings vehicles, but that's far from the reality. Withdrawals prior to retirement are commonplace, especially in tough economic times. One of the big banks looked into RRSP withdrawals a few years ago and here's what the results of its research indicated:

- Forty per cent of RRSP-holders had withdrawn money from their plan.
- The average number of withdrawals among those who had taken money out of an RRSP was three.
- The average amount taken out was $18,000.
- Almost half of those who made a withdrawal said they didn't intend to pay it back.

Common reasons for RRSP withdrawals include buying a home, paying down debt and covering day-to-day expenses.

The only one of these reasons that makes any automatic sense is the third, and we'll assume here that financial catastrophe has brought someone to the point where they're cashing in their retirement savings as a matter of survival.

One of the most popular reasons for raiding an RRSP is actually government-sanctioned. Through the Home Buyers' Plan, first-time buyers can withdraw up to $25,000 tax-free from an RRSP to buy a first home for themselves or someone with a disability (read about why using the Home Buyers' Plan is not a great idea in Chapter Seven). Another federal government program that allows you to remove money from an RRSP without paying taxes is the Lifelong Learning Plan. The idea is to use your RRSP savings as a source of funds for upgrading your education or training, or that of your spouse or common-law partner. There's a case to be made for this if the extra education will significantly boost your earning power and theoretically give you the income to increase your retirement savings.

As for the third most common reason for RRSP withdrawals, paying down debt, there are better ways to accomplish this very worthwhile objective. Try refinancing your mortgage, a consolidation loan or getting some budgeting help from a credit counselling agency. There are also some short-term practical reasons for not scooping money from your RRSP. Withdrawals are subject to withholding taxes (taken off the top of your withdrawal) of between 10 and 30 per cent, depending on how much you take and the province where you live. If you're in a higher tax bracket, you should expect that the withholding tax won't be enough to cover all the tax you owe on your withdrawal. Remember, the withdrawal amount is added to your annual income.

TAX-FREE SAVINGS ACCOUNTS VS. RRSPs FOR RETIREMENT SAVINGS

Pick one or the other, and then contribute to it regularly. Really, that's all you need to know, because actually saving for retirement is much more important than making the right choice between tax-free savings accounts and RRSPs. You will not be poor in retirement because you chose the TFSA instead of the RRSP, or vice versa.

That said, one or the other may be a better fit for your personal circumstances. So let's get to know the TFSA a little better and then compare it to the RRSP. TFSAs (some people pronounce this TIF-sas) were introduced in 2009, which means they're still a relatively new addition to the selection of government-sponsored savings vehicles. Let's review a few basics:

- Anyone aged 18 and older can contribute to a TFSA.
- The contribution limit started at $5,000 annually and was to rise in $500 increments as required by the level of inflation.
- Unused contribution room can be carried forward.
- No tax refund is generated by a TFSA contribution, but all gains generated by money invested or saved in one of these accounts are tax-free.
- You can use a high-interest savings account for your TFSA, you can use mutual funds or term deposits sold

by a bank, or you can have an account with a financial adviser or brokerage firm (full service or online) that allows you to hold a wide variety of investments.

- You can withdraw money from a TFSA anytime without penalty, and you're free to replace the money as long as you follow this rule: you can't contribute more than your unused contribution room in any one year, even if you make a withdrawal.

Ideally, any working adult would contribute to both RRSPs and TFSAs, and to registered education savings plans as well. Ideally, the Toronto Maple Leafs would be a perennial Stanley Cup contender, gas would stay below $1 per litre forever and we'd have world peace. Living in the real world is sometimes about hard realities and compromises, however, so let's look at RRSPs and TFSAs on the assumption you're not making enough to max out a contribution to both in every year.

I should point out here that I have come across young adult go-getters who have landed good jobs out of school and are making the maximum annual contribution to both TFSAs and RRSPs. It can be done. With a good starting salary and no children or house to maintain, it's not unthinkable to maximize your savings. Before we delve into the matter of TFSAs vs. RRSPs, it's first worth noting that there is no flat-out "wrong" approach, and nor is there a universal correct strategy. All you can do is understand how both RRSPs and TFSAs work and then develop a strategy based on your personal situation.

First, let's review the retirement savings landscape in Canada. The key features are:

- **Old Age Security.** A federal program designed to provide a modest source of retirement income at age 65 for people who have lived in Canada for at least ten years after turning 18; at higher income levels, the federal government starts clawing back some of your OAS benefits, and they can disappear altogether if you're a well-off retiree.
- **Guaranteed Income Supplement.** A federal top-up of OAS for low-income seniors.
- **Canada Pension Plan.** People who earn a salary and are over 18 will have CPP premiums taken off their paycheque to provide for pension benefits in retirement; the amount of the premiums is based on salary, as are CPP payouts.
- **Company pensions.** There are different types of pension plans, but the common theme is that you and your employer will put money into an organized investment plan each time you're paid; when you retire, you will receive a monthly income based on various criteria (read on in this chapter for more on pensions).
- **Personal savings.** RRSPs, TFSAs and other amounts held in non-registered accounts.

If you're in a low-income bracket in your working years, you may be able to get along okay in retirement with some combination of OAS, CPP and GIS. More likely, OAS and CPP will create a savings foundation on which you will add one or more of company pensions, RRSPs and TFSAs.

Obviously, RRSPs and TFSAs become much more important if you don't have a company pension.

Now, back to RRSPs vs. TFSAs. To frame this debate, let's say our goals are to save as much as possible for retirement and pay as little as possible in taxes. Research by Jamie Golombek, managing director of tax and estate planning with CIBC Private Wealth Management, has found that RRSPs and TFSAs can produce the same results as savings vehicles. Assume you're in a 40 per cent tax bracket and you decide to take $5,000 of your pre-tax salary and put it into both a TFSA and an RRSP. After income tax is applied to your TFSA contribution, you're left with $3,000. With the RRSP, your contribution of $5,000 will result in tax savings of 40 percent, which means you will not lose $2,000 to taxes up front and you will be able to save the full $5,000 in your RRSP.

If you earned investment returns of 5 per cent over the next twenty years, the $3,000 in the TFSA would grow to $7,960. Because TFSAs are tax-free, you'd get to keep the entire amount for yourself on withdrawal. In the RRSP, meanwhile, your $5,000 would have grown to a much fatter $13,266. But if we assume you're in the same 40 per cent tax bracket at the time you make your withdrawal after twenty years, you'd end up with the exact same amount as the TFSA produced—$7,960.

It's important to highlight the assumption made here that you're a disciplined saver. Remember how the $5,000 RRSP contribution was based on $5,000 in pre-tax money? You had $3,000 after taxes, and then topped it back up to $5,000 by adding the $2,000 in taxes the government refunded to you. You should know that many people would take that $2,000 and not put it back into the RRSP. Some would use it to pay down debt, which is certainly reasonable. Others would spend it in one way or another, giving themselves no value beyond immediate gratification (hey, we all need some of that from time to time). The point here is that if you spent the $2,000 refund in our example, you'd be pitting a $3,000 RRSP investment against a $3,000 TFSA investment. Given that taxes would still apply on the RRSP withdrawal after twenty years, the tax-free TFSA would produce by far the better result.

Another assumption we've made here is that you'd have the same tax rate in retirement that you do now, which may not be realistic. Right now, you're probably in the early phase of your career and far from your peak earning years. In fact, you may well be earning less now per year than you would in retirement. If that's the case, then your modest salary today is generating modest tax refunds on contributions to RRSPs. In retirement, your larger income would generate higher tax hits on RRSP withdrawals. See the tax mismatch here? It's the reason why TFSAs make sense for young adults who are just starting to save for retirement. Your TFSA contributions would be made with your net income, which reflects taxes paid at your current low rate. When you're in retirement and your income is presumably larger, your TFSA withdrawals are tax-proof.

Later on in life, you may decide to rethink your use of TFSAs and RRSPs. For example, you may decide you need a tax refund from an RRSP contribution for one purpose or another. Just remember that TFSAs generate tax-free, worry-free income in retirement, while RRSPs ensure that you and the taxman have a continuing relationship. One more point on this is that money pulled out of a TFSA won't affect your eligibility to receive full OAS benefits. Money from an RRSP is considered taxable income and thus could cause some or all of your OAS to be clawed back.

RRSPs & TFSAs: A TAX EXPERT'S VIEW

An edited transcript of a Q&A with Jamie Golombek.

You've been critical of what you describe as a fixation people have with the tax refund they get from RRSP contributions. Could you explain why?

People are so excited by this refund, but what is it, anyway? It's all about, "Do I want to pay tax now, or do I want to pay tax later?"

You're referring here to the fact that you'll have to pay tax when you take money out of an RRSP in retirement?

Right. The refund is a not a refund; it's a deferral of tax.

Isn't the obvious advice to maximize contributions to RRSPs and TFSAs?

Nearly all Canadians cannot afford to do both—they just don't have the money. So they need to make decisions.

What about the fact that it's easy to withdraw money from

a TFSA and essentially steal from your own retirement fund?

There's this idea that if I put money in an RRSP, at least psychologically I've got this fence. Even advisers are recommending to clients that they do the RRSP because it's earmarked for retirement. But 80 per cent of all RRSP withdrawals are done by people under age 60. (Note: This excludes withdrawals for the Home Buyers' Plan and the Lifelong Learning Plan.)

You highlight TFSAs for young adults because they won't get much of a tax refund for an RRSP contribution, and they'll quite likely be in a higher tax bracket in retirement. Are RRSPs to be avoided by young adults, then?

The message I don't want to get out there is that RRSPs are bad. Because they're not. RRSPs are still a great way to save, and an important part of almost every Canadian's portfolio.

For parents, where do RESPs fit in?

I would say RESPs before anything else, if there's any remote chance that your children might attend some type of post-secondary education.

TFSAs AS GIFTS

A nice thing about the TFSA, from your parents' point of view, is that they don't have to worry about attribution rules, which stipulate that investment gains on money given to someone as a gift are attributed back to the person who gave the gift. Put simply, your parents can give you money to put in your tax-free savings accounts without any tax considerations for them or you (remember, you must be 18 or older to have a TFSA).

Let's say your parents are in the fortunate position of having made the maximum contribution to your registered education savings plan, and they're looking to put additional money away on your behalf. One option would be to set up a TFSA for you and park the extra contributions there. Or maybe it looks like you won't go to college or university. RESPs are tricky in this situation (see Chapter One), but TFSAs have no strings attached. You can use the money in a TFSA set up on your behalf for whatever purpose, and it's tax-free.

Grandparents may also find TFSAs useful as a way to help their grandchildren afford university. It's possible for grandparents to set up a registered education savings plan, but it just might be that a TFSA is a better idea. Ideally, you could end up with an RESP set up by your parents and a TFSA set up by your grandparents. That's a versatile package of savings to help you through school and beyond.

A FEW FINAL POINTS IN FAVOUR OF RRSPs

Let's make sure that you know about a few miscellaneous benefits of registered retirement savings plans that haven't been covered so far:

- Spousal RRSPs: You can contribute to an RRSP for your spouse and receive the tax refund yourself.

- Pension splitting: As a retiree, you can pull money out of an RRSP and attribute it to a spouse with a lower income, thereby equalizing your taxes.
- No withholding taxes on U.S. stock dividends: A Canada–U.S. tax treaty allows Canadians to receive dividends from U.S. corporations without the usual withholding tax being applied by the Internal Revenue Service.

AN INTRODUCTION TO PENSION PLANS FOR THOSE LUCKY ENOUGH TO FIND JOBS OFFERING THEM

Salary, health benefits and number of vacation days—these are your big concerns when evaluating the compensation paid by a first job. Don't forget to look for a company pension, though. While it's utterly irrelevant to life in your twenties and thirties, it's a building block of a financially comfortable retirement.

The most desirable type of pension is the defined benefit plan, in which your employer promises to pay you a defined amount of money per month in retirement, based on your age, years of service with the company and salary. Notice what's missing here? It's the idea of returns being based on stock and bond market returns. With a defined benefit plan, your employer assumes the risk that the markets will tank and thereby reduce your retirement savings.

You may just luck into a defined benefit plan if you work for a big corporation or for government. But in the broader employment world, defined benefit pensions are in decline as a result of the burden they place on employers. They're being replaced in many cases with defined contribution plans, which are similar to defined benefit plans in that both you and your employer put set amounts of money into the plan. The difference is that your pension payments in retirement are determined by the performance of the products in which your pension money has been invested. If the stock market takes a fall before you retire, your savings could be hurt significantly in the immediate term at least.

Still another pension possibility is called the group RRSP, which is a basic retirement savings program into which an employer may or may not make contributions. A notable wrinkle with group RRSPs is that employer contributions are considered a taxable benefit. Employer contributions to defined benefit and defined contribution plans are not taxable. An offsetting benefit of the group RRSP is that employer contributions are immediately considered to belong to the employee. With traditional pensions, employer contributions "vest," or become the employee's property, after a period of time, often two years.

With both defined contribution plans and group RRSPs, you'll typically be offered a selection of mutual funds in which to invest. Ideally, these funds will be run by top money management firms and have significantly lower fees than you would get if you bought your own mutual funds through a bank or investment adviser. Also, there will no sales charge to buy them.

HOTLIST:
TEN THINGS YOU NEED TO KNOW ABOUT YOUR COMPANY PENSION PLAN

1. Should I join my company pension plan as soon as I can?

Yes, and this applies to any kind of pension to which your employer is making contributions. In essence, pension contributions by your employer are payments of salary set aside to help you in retirement. If you pass them up by declining to join the pension plan, you're missing out on part of your salary. Joining your pension right away also means you're starting to save for retirement. Even if you're not contributing to RRSPs, you've started the long task of providing for yourself in retirement. One other benefit of pension plans is that contributions are automatically made through payroll deduction. You'll never forget to contribute, or be unable to find the money. Note: Joining a company pension plan may be mandatory.

2. I don't expect to be at my job forever—what happens to my pension when I move?

You generally have a few options if you depart a company where you've participated in a pension plan. One is to leave your money in the pension until you retire and then collect whatever level of payments you're entitled to. Another is to transfer your pension holdings into a locked-in retirement account, or LIRA, which is very similar to an RRSP except for the fact that you can't easily access the money. It's essentially locked in until you retire (although you may be allowed access in cases of financial hardship). You may also be able to transfer your pension to your new employer's plan.

3. What are some other pension implications from changing jobs?

A defined benefit pension can be left where it is at your old employer until you retire and start drawing on it. The question you have to ask is whether your employer—and by extension the pension plan—is built for the long term and likely to be around decades from now when you retire. If you're skeptical, then have your money transferred into a LIRA.

If you have some good-quality funds in your defined contribution plan, you may not easily find better options outside the pension. That's an argument for leaving your money where it is. DC plans are often thought of as second best to defined benefit plans, but they can actually work well for people who expect to change jobs frequently. Unlike defined benefit plans, a defined contribution plan has nothing to do with time of service with the same employer.

4. I have a defined contribution plan—can I count on someone helping me make sure I'm managing it intelligently?

Short answer: no. DC plans put the onus on the employee to smartly manage his or her pension savings. This is a hugely important matter. If you make a bad decision and, say, keep your money sitting in a money market fund (safe but very low returns unless interest rates are sky high), you could effectively cheat yourself of much better returns. Conversely, too much risk through the years could leave you with little in the way of investment gains by retirement.

Ask your human resources department at work for some guidance on how to invest. Some companies are bringing in consultants to run workshops for employees on how to invest in DC plans.

5. With my DC plan, can I set it and forget it?

Again, no. You'll want to make the mix of funds in the plan more conservative as you get closer to retirement. In the early years after you start in the pension, you may also find that you're able to tolerate more—or less—stock market exposure that you initially thought. You may also find that as you get older and more knowledgeable about investing, you'll want to take a fresh look at your pension holdings and make adjustments.

6. What questions should I ask about the investment choices for the funds in my DC plan or group RRSP?

You could ask who's running the funds, but the names won't mean much to you. You simply want to establish that veteran pension fund managers are handling things. Fees are another question—you want to establish that you're paying very low fees, which will put you in a position to reap greater returns. Fees are taken off the top of fund returns (returns are virtually always reported to you with fees deducted), so lower fees are better. A website like Globeinvestor.com can help you get some context on fee trends for various mutual fund categories. Note: Your human resources department should have a brochure that explains your fund choices.

7. What funds should I use?

For a properly diversified portfolio, you'll want exposure to bonds, Canadian stocks, U.S. stocks and global stocks. Your exact mix will depend on your age, your goals and your stomach for stock market risk, but a quick-and-dirty mix for a 30-year-old would be 70 to 80 per cent in stocks and the rest in bonds. The easy solution: look for a balanced fund, which will include both stocks and bonds. Money market funds are okay for a small portion of your holdings—say, 5 per cent. If interest rates are high, then money market funds are more attractive.

8. How will I know how I'm doing?

You'll get annual statements—be sure to read them. Defined benefit pensions will tell you how much in monthly retirement benefits you're eligible to receive based on your personal details. DC and group RRSP statements focus on how your investments are doing. Details can sometimes be sketchy on your statements, but at very least you'll be able to see how you're doing this year compared to last year. Ideally, you'll get an average annual return since you started contributions.

If we estimate long-term inflation at 2.5 per cent, then you'll need to make more than that just to break even on a real-world basis where costs are steadily rising. A balanced fund making 5 to 6 per cent annually is doing a pretty good job.

9. Is my pension bulletproof?

Defined benefit plans are only as solid as the financial status of the pension fund itself. The key is how well the plan is funded. Fully funded is ideal, but underfunded isn't a worry as long as your employer has the where-withal to add more money. When a weak company goes bankrupt with an underfunded pension, employees and pensioners can end up with less money in retirement income than they expected.

Defined contribution funds and group RRSPs are invested in funds that are kept separate from the assets of both your employer and the financial firm that offers them. So even if they go under, your investments should remain separate and safe. Then you've only got financial market risk to worry about.

10. Will my company look after my best interests in managing the pension plan?

No. The company will look after its own best interests. Employees must remain vigilant. Pension matters are boring and hard work to understand, but they're as much a part of your compensation as your dental benefits, vacation pay and salary.

CHAPTER FIVE SUMMARY

1. **First things first—get that debt paid down.** Debt paydown is your top priority when you start your first job, although it doesn't have to entirely crowd out retirement saving.

2. **It's never too early to start retirement planning.** You're entitled to enjoy yourself when you start drawing a serious salary, but long-term financial thinking should start immediately.

3. **Compare RRSPs and TFSAs.** There's no categorically wrong choice, but one could work better for you than the other based on your personal situation. TFSAs can make sense for young workers with modest salaries.

4. **Get on a regular savings plan.** Whether you use an RRSP or TFSA to save for retirement, get on a regular plan where money is automatically transferred in from your chequing account each month or every time you get paid.

5. **Pension plans rule.** If your company has a pension plan, jump on it as soon as you can.

SIX

MOBILITY: OR, CARS AND YOU

Anyone who knows me will be surprised to hear my advice on buying a car: put it off for as long as possible.

In my first few years in the workforce, I bought a car and then traded up every couple of years or so. I lived in a modest bachelor apartment, but I always had a two-seat sportscar sitting in the parking spot that went along with it. The amount I spent on car payments was, to me, an excellent value because I loved cars (an inherited trait on my dad's side). But from a purely financial point of view, I wasted serious money on car payments that could have gone to other things like retirement savings.

I'm here to tell you: do not do what I did.

In this chapter, we'll look at the emerging options for people who need a car periodically but don't want to own one. For those who *must* buy a car, we'll also look at ways to make the vehicle-buying process as inexpensive as possible.

RETHINKING THE CAR

Cars offer mobility, status and independence, so you may have it in mind to get one as soon as you can. Hold up, though. While you will almost certainly need a car when you start a family, you may find that you'll be able to do without your own set of wheels in your early working years after you graduate.

What's so great about the car-free life? Let's start with the idea that cars are wealth destroyers. I'm a car guy, remember, not some tree-hugging enviro-zealot who thinks everyone should be dashing around town on bikes and rickshaws. But I feel duty bound to point out that you'll get off to a much stronger financial start in life as an adult without having to buy and maintain a car.

Here's a quick roundup of costs car owners face:

- **Purchase price.** Even the cheapest car models these days go for $13,000 to $15,000, and that's for a stripped-down version without sales taxes or miscellaneous fees.
- **Financing costs in the form of interest charged on loans or leases.** You could easily pay a rate of between 5 and 10 per cent.
- **Gasoline.** Prices are going up all the time; if you're thinking of driving a hybrid, the cost of buying could approach $30,000.
- **Oil changes, tune-ups and required maintenance.** Basic oil

changes run about $40 or so, and tune-ups can cost anywhere from $150 to $500.

- **Annual licence renewal.** At least $65 to $75 per year.
- **Insurance.** Depending on what kind of car you own and its age, you could easily pay between $750 and $1,000— or more.
- **Parking both where you live and at work.** A parking spot at your apartment or condo means a hefty surcharge on your monthly rent or mortgage payment; parking spots downtown are extremely pricey.

Putting aside the purchase price of a car, we're talking here about thousands of dollars per year. That's money you could otherwise use to pay off your student loans faster, start up an emergency fund and build a retirement savings foundation. You have to plan for the car-free life, though. If you're looking for a place to live, consider something close to public transportation. And don't live so far away from work that you're stuck with massively long commutes by bus.

INTRODUCING THE CAR-SHARING SERVICE

Perfect for city dwellers, the car-sharing service offers access to a vehicle on an as-needed basis. Zipcar, a car-sharing service that was active in Toronto and Vancouver as this was being written, says its members have reported saving more than $600 per month over owing their own vehicles.

A variety of packages are available for car sharing, but the general principle is that you sign up to join a service and then book a vehicle online or by phone when you need one. Cars can be picked up and dropped off at strategic locations throughout major cities, many of them near public transit. You're charged by the hour or day and should expect to pay more at high-demand periods. There are also sign-up fees and annual fees, but they tend to be nominal. Zipcar, for example, charges a $30 application fee and $65 annually; hourly rates range from $8.75 to $12, and daily rates from $77 to $83.

Now for what you *don't* have to pay: insurance, repairs and gas (there may be fuel surcharges if you travel beyond a certain distance). The bottom line is that you're paying to use a car, not to own one.

LEARN MORE ABOUT CAR SHARING

Car Sharing Canada	www.carsharing.ca
CarSharing.net	www.carsharing.net
Transport Canada	www.tc.gc.ca/eng/programs/environment-utsp-carsharing-1068.htm

Two alternatives to car sharing are carpooling and ride sharing, both of which can be arranged online. One option is PickUpPal (pickuppal.com), which is an online tool that matches people seeking rides with those who are already going somewhere. This is a useful service for students (as well as anyone else who needs a ride). Other ride-sharing or carpooling resources are eRideShare.com and Carpool.ca.

For weekend trips, consider renting a car. Reward

yourself for your everyday car-free lifestyle by renting something nice for a few days.

BIKES ARE GREAT, TOO

Here's an idea: instead of getting yourself into debt buying a crummy used car, why not pay cash for a great bike (and helmet)? If you live and work in the city, a bike can take care of your commuting and some of your other transportation needs. Bike upkeep costs are negligible—no gas, no insurance, no oil changes—and you never pay to park.

OKAY, YOU STILL WANT A CAR

The frugal view on car buying is to go with a used vehicle because new cars are for suckers. The rationale here relates to depreciation, or the steady decline in the value of cars bought new. It's said that a new vehicle loses up to 20 per cent of its value the moment it leaves the dealer's lot. The depreciation rate slows in the next few years, but the lesson here is clear. If you buy a used car, you avoid that big upfront drop in value and have the opportunity to buy a nearly new vehicle at a much-reduced price.

Now, let's play devil's advocate with the buy-used approach. For one thing, the used-car market can be very competitive if you're targeting a reliable, sought-after vehicle. If you find what seems to be an attractive used car that's just a year or two old, be sure to compare what it would cost to buy the same model new. Another consideration is the potential cost of repairs. New vehicles typically come with a bumper-to-bumper warranty that runs for at least three years. Some companies may offer full coverage for longer periods, and most offer five years of power-train coverage (engine, transmission and some related components). Still, it's a general rule that the older the used car you're buying, the more vulnerable you are to surprise repair bills. And don't forget the cost of routine maintenance for even very reliable used vehicles. New tires, new brakes or a new timing belt can easily cost upward of $500.

There are some intangible factors as well when deciding whether to go new or used, like the pleasure of driving something brand new and being able to get exactly the model you want with precisely the options you like. Ultimately, though, the decision for many young adults will come down to how much money they have and their willingness to take on debt.

Let's be clear here: most people will have to borrow to buy even a used car, unless they're purchasing a clunker. While writing this, I checked the AutoTrader.ca website to look for used Honda Civics, which are great cars (my wife and I have owned a couple over the years). I found a five-year-old model with a low 65,056 kilometres on it. The cost was $8,997, which would be higher once you add taxes.

CAN YOUR PARENTS HELP YOU DRIVE A HARD BARGAIN?

Buying cars intelligently is one of those skills you learn by doing, which is to say you'll probably make some costly mistakes before you get the hang of it. The auto industry thrives on unsavvy buyers—don't be one of them. If your parents know a reputable dealer they've dealt with before, get them to introduce you and then sit in on the negotiations. Use the fact that your parents have bought from this dealer before as leverage for a good deal.

If you're buying a used car, see if your parents can arrange to have the vehicle inspected at a garage they trust. A whole series of my early used cars were economically inspected before purchase and then kept on the road by a mechanic my dad used.

GET YOUR GRAD DISCOUNT

Many car companies offer rebates for recent graduates buying new vehicles. As this book was written, for example, Mazda offered recent university and college grads $500 for its less expensive models and $750 for pricier vehicles. Basically, Mazda would apply this money against the final selling price of the vehicle.

Nissan's grad program offered anywhere from $350 to $500, as well as four free oil changes in the first year, while General Motors offered savings of up to $750. Whatever car company you're dealing with, ask for a grad discount and then be prepared to provide verification that you've completed your course of study. One other tip is not to mention your grad status until after you've struck the best deal possible. Salespeople may not be as willing to cut the price of a car if they know you've already got a discount in your back pocket.

BUYING VS. LEASING

Leasing is like buying the use of a car for a set period of time, usually two to four years. You'll typically kick in a down payment of up to a few thousand dollars—zero-down leases are sometimes possible—and then make monthly payments. At the end of the lease, you either walk away or buy the vehicle outright for a predetermined price.

The benefit of leasing is that even with a small down payment, your monthly payments will typically be lower than if you took out a loan to buy a vehicle. Remember, when you buy, you're financing the entire cost of the vehicle, and you'll eventually own it. With leasing, you're financing only a few years' worth of use. Leasing means you'll almost certainly be driving a new vehicle more often than if you bought. If you lease for three years, you'll also have the comfort of knowing your vehicle is fully covered by the manufacturer's bumper-to-bumper warranty. You'll pay routine maintenance costs, of course, but there shouldn't be any surprise repair bills.

With the average new car price somewhere in the range of $25,000 in Canada, leasing is bound to sound attractive to young adults just starting out in the workforce. But over the long term, buying is better than leasing because you'll eventually pay off your car loan and get out from under those monthly payments. Leasing successive vehicles means perpetual payments for vehicles that you never own. Three other negatives to leasing:

- There are limitations on the amount of mileage you can put on a vehicle without incurring extra charges.
- Normal wear and tear is okay, but you'll have to pay to fix any more serious damage when you return your leased vehicle. (I've heard of bills in the thousands of

dollars for cars coming off a lease.)
- You can't modify the vehicle in any way.

THE LAST WORD ON CARS

Here's the optimum balance of smart financial management and convenience when it comes to cars. Stay car-free as long as possible after you graduate and then acquire a car around the time you plan to start a family (you might even need two if you have a family with two working parents). Your driving years will last right through your working life and into retirement—grandparents need cars, too—and then taper off as you age. Seniors living in cities with good public transportation links may find that car-sharing services and rentals are an adequate replacement for owning cars. Reasons for avoiding cars are piling up—rising fuel prices, environmental concerns and the lack of both will and funding in many cities for expanding the network of roads and highways to accommodate more cars. There's a personal finance argument as well. No car = more money for you.

CHAPTER SIX SUMMARY

1. **Rethink the car.** Do you really need a car in your young and single years with alternatives like car-sharing services becoming available?
2. **Cost it out.** The financial commitments of owning a car go far beyond the payments—there's maintenance, licensing, gas and insurance as well, and all these costs keep rising.
3. **Be a smart buyer.** Remember the grad discount that many car companies offer.

CASE STUDY: Laura

Laura, 25, grew up in Ottawa, attended university in London, Ontario, and ended up living in Vancouver, where she works as an engineer in the natural resources industry. Her intensive studies in chemical engineering and business enabled her to land a job with a starting salary of $50,000 (within a few years she was up to $75,000). That in turn has helped her start an aggressive savings program, first, to buy a home in the pricey Vancouver market and, second, to provide for her retirement.

Estimated total education costs: $115,000.

Amount of student loans: $10,000.

Total amount repaid to date: $10,000.

Primary source of funding: I had very supportive parents, I received a few scholarships and I had excellent summer jobs. All of these combined allowed me to graduate with minimal educational debt. The money I borrowed was used during my fourth year of university, when I completed a foreign exchange in England.

Hopes to buy a house by: 2015.

City of choice: Vancouver.

Target down payment: 25 per cent.

Amount saved to date: $50,000.

Percentage of take-home pay being saved: 20 per cent on average.

Savings vehicles used: RRSP, TFSA, non-registered investment account.

What's your biggest financial mistake as a young adult? When I first graduated and moved to B.C., I was so sick of living like a student that I wanted the best of everything. I probably spent too much money on furniture and clothes during my first year of employment. I had a line of credit that was available for emergencies, and I ended up using it to pay my Visa bill one month. At that point, I realized I needed to improve my budgeting skills.

Best piece of financial advice to other young adults: Automatic deductions for savings are the easiest way to "pay yourself first." You can't spend the money if you never see it in your daily account.

Best financial advice for students still in school: I was very lucky to have such supportive parents, so I had minimal debt during school. However, I did contribute to my education by working during my summer holidays. During the summer before I went to England, I had four jobs: a full-time engineering job, lifeguarding, waitressing and tutoring. I worked *a lot* that summer, but I made good money and I was able to travel Europe more than was originally planned. Good summer jobs and saving during those summer months was crucial for me to leave school with minimal debt.

Financial lessons my parents taught me: The more I think about it, the more I realize how much my parents taught me through their own actions. My mother never buys anything unless it's on sale. My father will always do the maintenance around the house and on the vehicles. Even though they both had very secure and well-paying jobs, we never spent much money as a family. There was a balance, though; we did go on some nice vacations, so it was good to see that being frugal every day could lead to a little extra money during holidays.

SEVEN

BUYING A HOME

Who doesn't think buying a house is one of the few total no-brainers in personal finance? Houses appreciate in value, sometimes at rates that make the stock market look comatose. At worst, a house is a forced savings plan that shows its value later in life, after you're retired and are ready to downsize. You'll sell your house, take away a big chunk of tax-free money and use it to top up your retirement savings. This is the conventional wisdom on why buying a house is a great thing, and it's just begging to be challenged. That's the point of this chapter. I fully expect most readers will buy a home, and they'll be well prepared to do it after reading the next several pages. But at least they'll go in with a much clearer understanding that our national obsession with houses as an investment is potentially destructive.

OUR HOUSING OBSESSION

It's hard to think of an adult rite of passage as universally and enthusiastically supported as buying your own home (house or condo). People of all income levels and cultural backgrounds want to own a home. There is no influential anti-home ownership faction to be found anywhere.

There are lots of reasons for this, the first being that it's a basic human instinct to want your own space. There's the greed aspect—houses have been unbelievably good investments in some cases, and new buyers have hopes of making out similarly well. Housing is also a huge part of the economy, so it's naturally looked upon favourably. Home ownership is also a value pushed by governments. That's why we had thirty-five- and forty-year mortgages for a while here in Canada, and why zero-down mortgages were briefly allowed. Houses were getting expensive and people needed help to buy them. The government delivered.

Renting a home has . . . well, a low-rent feel to it. It suggests impermanence, shiftlessness, a sense of settling for second best. It's an uninformed prejudice that we would do well to get over because it's preventing people from making smart decisions about whether buying or renting is a better option.

HOTLIST:
THREE MONEY MYTHS ABOUT HOUSES

• **Houses are always a good investment.** People usually say this after a stretch of years in which house prices have soared, just as they get excited about stocks after a few good years for the markets. Houses *can* be a good investment, but a lot depends on when you buy and where you buy. Big, growing cities are better than small industrial towns in decline. That said, you can lose money in big cities, too. When my wife and I were looking for our first home in Toronto back in the early 1990s, we viewed several houses put on sale by people who had paid top dollar in the late 1980s and then watched the value of their home plunge below what they owed on their mortgage. Between April 1989 and February 1996, the average resale home price in Toronto fell to $192,406 from $280,121, a drop of 31 per cent.

- **It's smart to buy as much house as you can afford.** Building on the previous myth, this old bit of nonsense is based on two often erroneous ideas: one, that bigger houses are always better; two, that your house will become more affordable over time (ignoring such matters as slow wage growth, inflation and the cost of having kids).

- **Your house will pay for your retirement.** The thinking here is that you'll sell your house for a big whack of tax-free money (you generally pay no tax when selling your principal residence), carve off a piece to buy a condo or a cute little bungalow and then invest the rest to pay for a carefree retirement. The flaw in this plan? So many people have done this that the price of condos and cute little bungalows has soared. You'll probably have some money left over when you sell the family home and downsize, but it won't be a big factor in your retirement savings.

THE R-WORD (RENTING)

Buying a home is the best move for the most people. Not from a financial point of view necessarily, but because of the quality of life. Raising kids in a nice house in a pleasant neighbourhood near good schools is, for many people, a big part of what defines a life well lived.

If you can comfortably afford a house—and we'll look at that in more depth shortly—then I suggest you think hard about buying one. Certainly, your parents and friends will think it's the right move. But if you can't afford a house, or if you're uncomfortable with the financial load you'll have to carry as a homeowner, then please give renting some thought, because it could save you from financial hell.

As I wrote this, the housing market in Canada was just coming off a ten-year period in which prices had appreciated at an average annual rate of 8.3 per cent, enough to turn a home bought for $300,000 into one worth $665,895. Very few first-time buyers were able to buy anything without choosing the maximum thirty-year amortization, and even minimum 5 per cent down payments were a struggle to put together in many cities. The only thing keeping the housing market going was low interest rates, a temporary stimulant applied by the Bank of Canada to support the economy.

Higher interest rates were inevitable back then; the only question was when increases would start kicking in. Higher rates make houses more costly—surprisingly so. In fact, higher rates can have more of an impact on affordability than falling prices.

At the time of writing, the national average house price was $344,550. With a five-year fixed-rate mortgage at 3.9 per cent and a 10 per cent down payment, you'd be looking at payments every two weeks of $823 (includes mortgage loan insurance and a twenty-five-year amortization). Now let's jump forward a year and imagine that rates have climbed a full percentage point and prices have fallen 5 per cent. You're now buying a $327,322 house and taking a five-year mortgage at 4.9 per cent. The new biweekly payment: $865, which plays out to $5,460 or so more in total payments over the five-year mortgage term.

If interest rates are on the rise, then rushing into the market to avoid still-higher rates down the line seems the right move. The same logic can be applied to a market where prices are soaring. You may feel you have to dive in and claim a house you can barely afford or you'll never get into the market. I understand that psychology of rushing to buy, but it's not the right move unless you can properly afford to buy. If you lack the financial muscle to buy, then rent until you do.

Too often, the buy-vs.-rent argument is framed as if you'll be renting in perpetuity. I prefer to think of renting as a short-term option for people who cannot comfortably afford to be homeowners. Rent, live frugally so you can build your down payment and then make your move. Don't buy before you're ready, because owning a house is more expensive than you think (we'll look at all the various costs of buying and owning in a moment).

It's worth a quick look at renting permanently instead of buying. For a few reasons, I think the renting option is a mistake for many people.

- They miss out on the forced savings of making mortgage payments that gradually increase their equity in an asset they can later sell tax-free.
- They miss out on eventually paying off their mortgage and being able to live without fixed monthly housing costs (rent or mortgage payments).
- Finally, they severely limit their choice of places to live by looking only at rental properties.

The big knock on renting is that you're throwing money away—making your landlord richer instead of yourself. Renting is a fair bit cheaper than owning, though. While rents and mortgage payments can be comparable in some markets, the renter avoids paying property taxes and home maintenance costs. This creates an opportunity for the renter to gain back some ground against homebuyers. It's all about taking an amount of money equivalent to property taxes plus upkeep and putting it away. Short-term renters could save this differential to build up the down payment they'll use when they finally buy. Long-term renters could invest the differential for the long term. When they retire, this investment portfolio would be a rough equivalent to the money longtime homeowners get from selling their houses. Note: I've played around with quite a few rent-vs.-buy online calculators (a Google search will certainly find a bunch for you), and they generally indicate that buying nets you more money than a combination of renting and investing over the long term.

MORE THOUGHTS ON RENTING

Very gradually, the idea of renting is starting to get some traction with people in the financial community, especially in the United States. One example is Robert Shiller, the Yale professor who foresaw the collapse of the U.S. housing market last decade and who in early 2011 was warning that housing prices in certain Canadian cities looked overheated. In an interview with a *National Post* reporter, Shiller said he believed it made more sense for most people to rent and put the savings in a diversified portfolio. "People should think of buying a home as risky. They should maybe put some money in housing, but invest all over."

Another voice in favour of considering the rental option comes from the firm TriDelta Financial, which is headed by an adviser I know named Ted Rechtshaffen. In a newsletter to clients not too long ago, TriDelta said: "The debate about owning vs. renting has raged for decades, and for good reason, as there are pros and cons for both. However, if considered purely from a financial perspective, there is a strong case against home ownership." At the time, prices in Toronto were high enough that it might have been possible to rent a better-than-average home for the same monthly cost as an owner would have paid for basic housing costs. You can see how this situation would put renters and owners on a similar footing. The owner would be building equity in the home through the principal-repayment portion of his mortgage payments, while the renter could have invested.

Let's dig a little deeper into the question of renting vs. buying by talking with Ted. Here's an edited transcript of our conversation:

What's your overall view on home ownership?
For tax reasons [capital gains on your house are tax-free] and quality-of-life issues, I like the idea of owning a home. The thing about home ownership is that it's the financial decision that is least about the spreadsheet.

But what about those spreadsheet issues? You've told me, for example, that your financial models have investments in the stock market appreciating at an average annual 6 per cent over the long term, while real estate gains 4 per cent.
Historically, the stock market will outperform the real estate market.

When does renting make sense?
If you think you might not be in a house for six or seven years.

What's your thinking on that?
It's very costly to do a real-estate transaction. Every time you buy and sell a house, you spend all this money to get it ready to put on the market. And then there are real estate

commissions, land-transfer taxes and other transaction costs.

You're saying that the cost of selling a house you've lived in for only a short while can nullify the financial benefits. But what about the costs of living in a home—what impact do they have on the question of renting vs. buying?
The societal pressure to own a house as soon as possible gets a lot of people to buy before they're really in a financial position to do it. They don't have money in case they lose their job, they don't have money to furnish half the rooms in their homes and they don't have money to go out to dinner. The question is, are you in financial shape to own a house? A lot of people are not.

HOW TO SAVE FOR A HOME
One option is to use a high-interest savings account held in a tax-free savings account. Since the advent of the TFSA in 2009, that's an intelligent way to save for a home. You can also draw from your registered retirement savings account using a federal government program called the Home Buyers' Plan.

House prices in larger cities are such that you'll probably need both your TFSA savings and the Home Buyers' Plan to scrape enough money together for a down payment. But if you're fortunate enough to have substantial savings, try not to dip into your retirement savings via the HBP.

Introduced in 1992 to help first-time buyers afford a house without a ginormous mortgage, the HBP allows you to withdraw up to $25,000 from an RRSP to use as a down payment on a first house. The HBP has been a source of RRSP withdrawals topping $15 billion and has greased the way for close to a million home purchases. My wife and I both used the HBP shortly after it was introduced to buy our first home in Toronto.

Taxes normally apply to RRSP withdrawals, but not in this case. Instead, plan users are put on a schedule of repaying the amount of their withdrawal gradually over a period of fifteen years (you can, of course, speed things up). If they don't make their scheduled annual payment in a particular year, the amount of the payment is added to their income.

The HBP is well enough known these days that I've had people ask me if they should contribute to an RRSP so they can withdraw money under the plan. Uh, no. You contribute to an RRSP to save for retirement. If you need some of your RRSP to afford a house, fine. But as noted in Chapter Five, there's too much of a tendency for people to see RRSPs as a savings account from which money can, if necessary, be withdrawn.

Ideally, RRSPs would be treated as untouchable until the day you leave the workforce. If you're together enough to put money in an RRSP as a young adult, why completely undermine this success by withdrawing the money? It's worth noting that the money you put in an RRSP early on is precious because of the power of compounding. A $2,000 RRSP contribution when you're twenty-seven would be worth $8,877.63 by the time you're sixty-five, assuming a very conservative average annual return of 4 per cent. At 5 per cent—still not an unrealistic number at all—you're looking at $12,770.95.

Why not just dispense with the idea of using RRSPs in favour of TFSAs to save for a down payment? The reason is that when you contribute to an RRSP, you generate a tax refund that can be reinvested into your retirement plan. It's like an instant guaranteed return on your RRSP contribution money, and it can give you a substantial lift in building your savings for retirement—or a down payment. If you're disciplined enough with your money to ensure that your tax refund goes back into your RRSP, then that's an argument for using it to fund your down payment. If you're not, and this describes most people, then a TFSA is as good as an RRSP to save for a home. In fact, a TFSA is arguably a better option in this case.

As you know from Chapter Five, people aged 18 and up can put a maximum of $5,000 annually in a TFSA (check to see if the limit has been increased), with contribution room starting to accrue as of 2009. Here are some advantages of the TFSA as a vehicle to save for a home:

- **Zero tax.** Whether you earn interest from a high-rate savings account or capital gains from trading stocks, the returns generated in a TFSA are tax-free.
- **Super-simple withdrawals.** There's paperwork involved in removing money from an RRSP under the Home Buyers' Plan, but a TFSA withdrawal can be done instantly and online, with the money transferred to your chequing account.

- **Payback flexibility.** The Home Buyers' Plan puts you on a rigid payback schedule, which is justifiable because it forces you to replenish your retirement savings; with TFSAs, you have lots of flexibility to pay as much or as little back as you want, when you want (subject to a restriction outlined in Chapter Five).
- **Your RRSP remains untouched.** While your TFSA goes to work for you in buying a home, your retirement savings get to quietly keep compounding for you.

Whether you're using a TFSA or an RRSP to save for a down payment on a home, you need to put safety first in your choice of investment. That's why I suggest you use a high-interest savings account and avoid anything to do with the stock market or even bonds. Canada's primary stock index, the S&P/TSX composite, averaged 8.3 per cent annually over the ten years to the writing of this book, including dividends. That's probably quite a bit better than you'll get with high-interest savings accounts, but what about the risk? In 2008, the composite index plunged 33 per cent. That's like saving $60,000 to buy a house and having the stock market turn it into not much more than $40,000.

Bonds can fall in price when interest rates rise, so avoid them as a down-payment savings vehicle as well. This leaves the high-interest account, which comes with deposit insurance for up to $100,000 when bought at a bank and is thus virtually bulletproof. The interest earned in a savings account is taxed like regular income, but you don't have to worry about that if you're using a TFSA or an RRSP.

THE FIRST-TIME HOMEBUYERS' TAX CREDIT

Introduced in 2009, this relatively new program to assist people with costs associated with buying a first home is much less well known than the Home Buyers' Plan. The HBTC is available to people who are buying a detached house, townhouse or condo. Here's the Canada Revenue Agency's explanation of how this tax credit will benefit you: The HBTC is calculated by multiplying the lowest federal income tax rate for the year by $5,000. If the lowest tax rate is 15 per cent, the credit will be $750. There's no need to send in any documents to prove your purchase, but keep them ready in case the tax people request them.

GETTING HELP FROM THE 'RENTS TO BUY A HOUSE

Your parents have quite possibly experienced a tremendous increase in the value of their home in the years they've lived there and raised a family. What a comfort to know all the money they have sunk into the place has generated real value. Let's hope they're enjoying this good fortune, because it's a big reason for the difficulties that twenty- and thirty-somethings are having in getting into the housing market.

This isn't about laying a guilt trip on your parents' generation. It's just a heads-up that their experience of buying a first home may be different from yours. As I wrote this, the average house price in Vancouver was just over $800,000, while Calgary was in the $400,000 range and Toronto was around $445,000. At these prices, down payments can take years and years to amass. This brings us to the question of whether it's a good idea to seek help from your parents to afford a home. The answer: a qualified yes.

Let's be clear: your parents do not owe you money to help with a down payment. Buying a home is a rite of passage for young adults, and ideally they will manage it by themselves, as generations before them did. But let's say your parents are comfortable enough financially to afford it and you're a long way from saving a decent down payment. A loan or gift at this juncture could pay off in the form of better financial health for you in the decades ahead. Having your parents top up a down payment means you get into the housing market faster, and that in turn means you will get your house paid off sooner. Adding a little heft to the down payment you've saved for yourself means you will need to borrow less.

Have your parents talked about helping you pay for a wedding? This is just a thought, but how about suggesting they convert that generous assistance into a chunk of money to be put toward a home? You could also suggest a loan, whereby your parents front you the money needed for a down payment and you repay it by a set period in the future.

A word of warning: your parents are not helping you if they assist you in buying a house that you cannot comfortably afford to live in and maintain.

CAN YOU AFFORD A HOUSE?

The best time to buy a house has nothing to do with forecasts for interest rates and housing. You're ready to buy when you can afford both a home and life's other financial commitments.

Let's examine the question of what it takes to afford a house. We'll start by looking from the perspective of the people who might lend you money to buy a home. They use two simple measures, the first of which is the gross debt service ratio, or GDS. The rule is that monthly housing costs, usually defined as mortgage payments (combined principal and interest) plus property taxes and heating, should not exceed 32 per cent of monthly household income before taxes.

The second measure is called the total debt service ratio, or TDS, and it compares pre-tax monthly income to housing costs plus monthly payments on lines of credit, credit cards and other debt. Housing costs plus debt payments shouldn't exceed 40 per cent of income. Both the GDS and TDS have been used for decades, sometimes with small variations. For example, some lenders will factor 50 per cent of condo fees into the calculation for the GDS, while solid borrowers might be allowed to take their TDS as high as 42 per cent.

In addition, lenders use what are commonly known as the "five Cs" to decide if someone can afford a mortgage: capacity to repay, which refers to income; collateral, or the value of the home; character, which factors in things like your record in repaying previous debts and how long you've been at your job; conditions, which refers to economic conditions; and capital, or the down payment.

All of this suggests that lenders are very careful and precise about who they'll lend to, and how big a mortgage they'll allow them to have. And yet, I'm almost certain that you'll be staggered by how much money you'll be allowed to borrow when you go in to discuss a mortgage with someone at your financial institution or a mortgage broker.

In fact, debt service ratios are not designed to protect borrowers from taking on too much mortgage. You could easily fall on the acceptable side of the GDS and TDS and still find it hard to meet all your monthly household expenses and savings goals. Lenders can live with this because they know human nature. When juggling all kinds of debts and expenses, people almost always put the mortgage first.

One way to attack the question of how much you can afford is to ensure that your housing-related debts come in well below the ceilings set out in the GDS and TDS. Another is to take a different approach suggested by Jeff Schwartz, executive director of the nonprofit Consolidated Credit Counselling Services of Canada. His opinion is that all housing costs, including mortgage payments, property taxes and home insurance, should ideally amount to no more than 25 per cent of your take-home pay. In expensive markets, up to 30 or 35 per cent may be necessary.

One last note about the GDS and TDS: they're simple calculations that you can do on your own or by using online calculators. Try the following:

- www.fiscalagents.com/toolbox/worksheets/mtgDebt.shtml
- www.cmhc-schl.gc.ca/en/co/buho/hostst/hostst_002.cfm

EVERYDAY HOME ECONOMICS

You probably have a sentimental view of the family home, and you may well want to recreate that feeling of security when you settle down yourself. But as your parents can tell you from their years as homeowners, houses are money-removal machines as much as they are the cradle of family life. Houses make you poorer in ways you may never have imagined when you sat in the lawyer's office signing the documents that made your purchase official. Leaky roofs and basements, bad wiring, clogged plumbing, mould in the attic, cracked foundations, worn-out windows, used-up appliances . . . that's just a partial list of the kind of sudden expenses that can crop up when you own a house.

We can quickly dispense with any ideas you might have that affording a house will be as much of a breeze as paying your monthly rent. Think you might as well put that money into a mortgage payment and build some equity? Not so fast. The expenses of owning a home are a far heavier burden than paying rent.

The mortgage is the foundation of your fixed monthly expense list as a homeowner. On top of that, you will have to pay for utilities—heat, hydro, water and sewer, phone (home and cell), cable TV and Internet. Prospective home-buyers, your experience paying utility bills as a renter won't be of much use. Hydro costs for a one-bedroom apartment will be just a tiny fraction of those for a home. If you're looking for real-world numbers about monthly utility bills for homeowners, ask your parents.

Additionally, you may wish as a homeowner to put away money each week or month for property taxes and home insurance. Property taxes, paid to the city or town where you live, can easily range from $2,000 to $5,000 annually, while home insurance can cost $500 to $1,000 per year, depending on how much coverage you want.

These are the fixed costs of owning a home. Next come the periodic costs associated with maintaining a property. These include fixing such things as a leaky roof. Finally, there are the fully discretionary costs such as home decorating, electronics, appliances and landscaping. If your finances are in good shape, you'll be able to bear these non-fixed costs of home ownership through a mix of week-to-week cash flow and savings. Remember the emergency fund? Got to have one if you're a homeowner.

HOTLIST:
SEVEN KILLER COSTS OF HOME OWNERSHIP THAT WILL SURPRISE FIRST-TIME BUYERS

- **Property taxes.** As noted, they amount to several thousand a year. Worse, they tend to go up every year, unlike income taxes.
- **Home insurance.** We'll look at this in more detail in Chapter Nine, but home insurance is another cost that seems to go up every year.
- **Furniture.** You probably won't have enough to fill the home you're buying, and while you may think you can live with that, you'll inevitably buy stuff to fill in the gaps.
- **New windows.** If you bought an older home that needs updated windows, expect to pay between $500 and $3,000 per window, depending on how large they are.

- **Landscaping.** A few trees can cost hundreds, and then there's the cost of garden tools, a hose and sprinkler, a wheelbarrow and so on.
- **Calling a plumber.** Figure on $80 to $100 just to get the plumber to your house. Parts extra.
- **Calling an electrician.** More than the plumber.

HOW TO TELL WHEN YOU'RE READY TO BUY

Technically speaking, you're ready to buy when you can afford the minimum 5 per cent down payment. That's a pretty thin slice of equity to have in a home, so why not try to get yourself up to 10 per cent? Heck, if you're an industrious saver, go for 20 per cent and you'll save on mortgage default insurance.

First-time buyers are sometimes a bit hazy on what mortgage insurance is all about. It's not to protect you, the buyer; rather, it's a way for banks and other lenders to cover themselves against the risk that a customer will default on a mortgage loan. You, the buyer, will pay the premium for this insurance coverage through a lump sum that is usually added to the amount of your mortgage. The insurance is provided by the Canada Mortgage and Housing Corporation, a federal government agency, as well as by private companies. With a 5 per cent down payment, your mortgage insurance works out to 2.75 per cent of the purchase price; with a down payment of 10 per cent, your premium is 2 per cent.

You now see why I suggest that you build as big a down payment as possible. If you put down 5 per cent on a home costing $300,000, your mortgage insurance premium amounts to $8,250. Amortized over thirty years, that amount of additional mortgage debt will cost you about $6,000 in interest, assuming you pay every two weeks and have a constant interest rate of 5 per cent.

High prices for homes in major cities make it difficult to save a sizable down payment, which means mortgage default insurance will be part of the cost of doing business for many buyers. But if saving a little longer to build your down payment will shield you from mortgage insurance premiums, then try to do it.

The down payment is the most important savings milestone you'll need to reach in order to get into the housing market, but it's not the only one. You'll also need a whack of savings to cover what are known euphemistically as "closing costs": the seemingly endless series of small, medium and large charges the homebuyer is dinged for.

Mortgage default insurance is considered to be a closing cost, but it will be added to the amount you're borrowing on your mortgage. Costs you'll be responsible for paying on the close of your purchase include a land-transfer tax in several provinces that can amount to 0.5 to 2 per cent of the value of a property. Next, there are legal fees, which the real estate brokerage Royal LePage estimates at between $1,000 and $2,500. Other costs listed by Royal LePage include the following:

- **Provincial sales tax on your mortgage insurance premium (charged in some provinces):** Due on closing and not added to your mortgage.

- **Adjustments for property taxes and utility bills already paid by the person whose house you're buying:** Usually less than $1,000.
- **Title insurance:** $200.
- **Mortgage application fee:** Close to $200.
- **Home inspection:** $300.

Other costs you'll have to pay include the following:

- **Movers:** Several thousand dollars, or rent a truck and get your friends to help.
- **Utility hook-ups:** $100 to $200.
- **Appliances:** $500 to $1,000 or more each, with the number you buy depending in large part on which appliances the seller refuses to leave behind.

In total, Royal LePage suggests saving 1.5 per cent of the purchase price to cover closing costs. If you add land-transfer tax, you'll probably need closer to 3 per cent.

HOTLIST:
TOP MORTGAGE TIPS FOR FIRST-TIME HOMEBUYERS

One of the smartest people I've come across on the subject of home-buying is the Vancouver-based mortgage planner Robert McLister. His blog, Canadian Mortgage Trends (canadianmortgagetrends.com), is an absolute must-read for anyone who wants to know about the latest developments in mortgages. Here, McLister provides some guidance for people who are preparing to purchase a first home.

- **Shop till you drop (for rates, that is).** Better yet, use a mortgage planner to compare multiple lenders quickly. The average Canadian gets only 1.96 mortgage quotes before negotiating what is likely the biggest debt of their lives. Two quotes aren't enough. If a little more homework lowers your rate an extra one-tenth of a percentage point, that'll save almost $1,200 of interest over five years on a typical $250,000 mortgage.

- **Focus on term as well as rates.** Always ask your mortgage adviser for amortization schedules (showing their rate assumptions and total interest costs) to illustrate why they recommend a particular term. Term, by the way, is the length of your mortgage contract. Generally, the longer the term, the higher the rate.

- **Don't fixate on a five-year fixed mortgage.** Depending on the rate cycle, as many as two out of three Canadians choose five-year fixed mortgages. Yet one- to three-year terms and variable-rate mortgages have a big mathematical edge the majority of the time.

- **Keep your banker or broker honest.** Spend fifteen minutes to compare his or her quote against rate-aggregating websites such as Globeinvestor.com. Make sure the bank's quote is within one-tenth of a point of the best rate on the market.

- **Use rate holds to your advantage.** If you haven't started home shopping yet, get a four-month rate hold to protect against rising rates.

- **Consider a compromise if you can't choose between a fixed- and variable-rate mortgage.** The compromise comes in the form of a hybrid mortgage (part fixed and part variable). Just be sure to keep the term for each part equal (i.e., don't pair a three-year variable with a five-year fixed). If the terms of a hybrid are unequal, you'll be at the lender's mercy when negotiating the renewal rate of the shorter term. The lender knows you can't break the longer term without paying a penalty.

- **Go mobile.** If you deal with a bank directly, you'll usually get lower rates if you apply through a "mobile mortgage specialist" instead of through the branch. Mobile mortgage specialists often get better rate exceptions because banks consider them to be a lower-cost distribution channel.
- **Never pay for an appraisal if you're a well-qualified borrower.** Good banks and brokers always cover them on "prime" mortgages (for people with good credit histories).
- **Don't touch ten-year fixed mortgages.** Ten-year terms have been cheaper than two consecutive five-year terms only 10 per cent of the time. That's true going all the way back to 1967, when good five-year fixed-rate mortgage data first became available.
- **Expect the unexpected.** Everyone who commits to a mortgage should have four to six months' worth of liquid cash to cover living expenses in case of job loss, illness, family issues, etc.
- **Don't overpay for large prepayment privileges.** Only 12 per cent of Canadians make lump-sum prepayments. If you're not going to maximize your annual prepayment allowance, look for a mortgage with a lower rate in lieu of

large prepayment privileges.

- **Boost your down payment.** A larger down payment not only costs you less in mortgage interest, but also lets you save on default insurance premiums.
- **Pay as much as you can.** If you choose a variable-rate mortgage, make your payment the same as if you took a five-year fixed mortgage at a higher rate. You'll save hundreds, if not thousands, of dollars of interest over your term.

ARRANGING YOUR FIRST MORTGAGE

Before going out to look at houses, you should see your bank or a mortgage broker to get pre-approved. This means getting the official view on how much house you can afford (you won't be spending to the limit, *right?*) and, more important, reserving a mortgage rate. Lenders will typically hold rates for 90 to 120 days, which means you're insulated from rate increases for that period of time. Rate holds are especially important for buyers who are house hunting at a time of rising rates. Remember, an increase of even half a percentage point can add significantly to your mortgage payments. Note that in a falling-rate environment, you'll get the lowest rate up to the time of closing your deal— you're not locked into your reserved rate.

Prepare for the mortgage pre-approval process by spending a few minutes to check out the interest rate landscape. Three websites to help you do this are:

- **RateSupermarket.ca:** Includes rates at lenders that deal directly with the public and those that deal only through mortgage planners.

- **Cannex.com:** A good overview of the posted rates that banks and credit unions are offering.
- **Ratehub.ca:** Shows you the "best" rates available for each term and type of mortgage.

The obvious place to go for a mortgage is the bank where you have your chequing account and they presumably know a bit about you. When talking to a banker, ask for the posted mortgage rate (the "official" rate, which no person with even one functioning brain cell pays) and then the best discounted rate. Don't be surprised if the discounted rate you're offered is above the lowest rates you've found online. Simply show your banker these rates and see how close he or she will get to them.

Decades ago, banks had all the leverage over first-time buyers and would sometimes take a patronizing, take-it-or-leave-it attitude in offering a lame interest rate. Today, buyers have recourse in the form of mortgage brokers or, as they're more and more often being called, mortgage planners.

A mortgage planner doesn't represent a single financial institution. Instead, he or she works with dozens of lenders who offer a varied mix of rates and terms. You describe what you want in a mortgage and a planner will find you the best deal. Have no hesitations about dealing with a mortgage planner. In fact, there's no reason not to deal with a planner from the get-go, other than the fact that your bank branch will be more familiar to you.

If you do use a mortgage planner, Robert McLister suggests you look for someone who

- has been licensed for more than two years;
- has closed deals worth at least $10 million in the last twelve months;
- is on the "status" lists of multiple big lenders, which means she is eligible for the lowest rates from lenders;
- will compare rates and features from all lenders, including banks that don't deal through mortgage planners.

The lowest possible interest rate is your top priority in arranging a mortgage, and don't let anyone at the bank tell you different. With houses as expensive as they are in major cities, saving even half a percentage point on a mortgage can save you tens of thousands of dollars over the life of your mortgage.

There are ways to shave your mortgage rate a little bit lower even after you've negotiated what appears to be the best deal possible. One is to close your purchase within thirty to forty-five days of applying for the mortgage. Lenders like a quick close because it reduces the chances of them guaranteeing rates to clients that turn out to be below market rates when their purchases close. Another way to take a bit off your rate is to give up some prepayment privileges, which means flexibility to make extra mortgage payments that go directly against your outstanding mortgage balance.

On one hand, prepayments are important for new home-buyers. Mortgages are structured in such a way that payments over the first several years go mainly toward interest and only minimally toward principal. A few lump-sum payments in the early years of a mortgage can really make a difference in getting your mortgage paid off sooner and reducing the amount of interest you pay. But let's be realistic: most homeowners wobble a bit as they learn how to manage their budgets, and that means the chances of having enough cash to make a mortgage prepayment are slim.

Don't get me wrong—I'm all for hammering down your mortgage as quickly as possible. But if you're arranging a first mortgage and you don't see yourself having the cash flow to make prepayments, then use that to your advantage by trying for a lower rate.

THE GREAT DEBATE: VARIABLE OR FIXED RATE

First, some definitions. A variable-rate mortgage is, just as the name suggests, a floating-rate loan where the rate you pay is tied to the prime lending rate at the major banks (the rate for top customers). The banks take their cue in setting their prime rates from the Bank of Canada's overnight rate, which rises at times when the economy is surging and inflation is a threat, and falls when the economy sags. A fixed-rate mortgage has a locked-in rate for the entire term, which can range from one year to ten or longer. Five years is by far the most popular term.

The great thing about a variable-rate mortgage is that you'll usually start off with a significantly lower rate than if you took a fixed-rate mortgage. As I write this, variable-rate mortgages were going for 2.80 per cent, which was derived by taking the 3 per cent prime rate and applying a discount of 0.20 of a percentage point. By comparison, five-year fixed-rate mortgages with a very good discount were going for 3.50 per cent.

This is an unusually small spread between the variable and fixed rate. But you can still see here that the prime rate would have to rise a fair bit to get the cost of a variable-rate mortgage above the five-year fixed cost. Even if this did happen, you'd have the comfort of knowing that you would get relief as soon as your bank started lowering its prime rate again. People with fixed-rate mortgages only get a chance to lower their rate at renewal time.

The fixed-rate mortgage at its simplest: pay more, worry less. Think of it as a mortgage that comes with an extra-cost insurance policy against the kind of interest rate spikes we've seen a few times in the past several decades.

Now for the question of which way to go for your own mortgage. For experienced homeowners with a firm grip on their household cash flow, a variable-rate mortgage is arguably the way to go. For first-time buyers, there's a strong case to be made for a fixed-rate mortgage.

Quite possibly, your parents are big believers in variable-rate mortgages. Many longtime homeowners did fabulously well with variable-rate mortgages in the past decade because of a long-term trend of mostly falling interest rates. The decade ahead could be different, which is why the recent experience of parents who have owned homes and have come to love variable-rate mortgages may not be relevant to their kids.

As the global financial crisis and recession began to unfold late last decade, central banks around the world dropped interest rates to historic lows to stimulate economic growth. Ever heard of Newton's Third Law of Motion, which says that for every action there is an equal and opposite reaction? That's roughly the thinking of the people out there who worry about super-low interest rates snapping back hard over a period of years.

Variable-rate mortgage diehards will explain how studies over the years have shown that riding variable-rate mortgages up and down will almost always cost you less than fixed-rate mortgages. Fine, great and wonderful. Now let's look at things strictly from the point of view of twenty- and thirtysomething adults just getting into the housing market.

First off, there's the very real potential that Canada might eventually enter an extended period of rising rates. That's something we haven't seen in ages, by the way. Everyone's view of variable-rate mortgages has been coloured by the recent experience of falling rates. Second, there's the fact that many people are paying high prices in major cities across the country. This means they will have sizable mortgages with payments that would be seriously affected by a jump in interest rates. If you're in this group, and you're not confident about your ability to comfortably afford your payments on a variable-rate mortgage should rates rise, then go with the certainty of a fixed-rate mortgage. If you can roll with higher rates, then the variable-rate mortgage will very possibly save you money in the long run.

OTHER MORTGAGE DETAILS

Should you pay your mortgage monthly, biweekly or weekly? I say weekly, but not because you'll save a bunch on interest costs. In fact, making mortgage payments every week saves an inconsequential amount over what are known as accelerated biweekly payments—paying every two weeks, so that by year's end, you'll have paid twenty-six times. In essence, you'll be making what amounts to an extra month's payment each year and drastically reducing the amount of time it will take to pay off your mortgage. If you arranged a $250,000 mortgage and assumed a level rate of 5 per cent, you could reduce a twenty-five-year amortization period down to 21.4 years just by going with accelerated biweekly payments rather than monthly payments.

So why go weekly if there's little benefit in terms of paying the mortgage off sooner and thus saving on interest costs? It's all about cash flow. Rather than having big chunks of money withdrawn from your chequing account every two weeks, you'll have a smaller amount taken out each week. That way, it's a lot easier to make sure you've got enough in the bank to cover your mortgage.

Another consideration in setting up your mortgage is the amortization period, which means the length of time you expect to take to repay what you owe. A twenty-five-year amortization period used to be standard, but then the federal government allowed buyers the option of taking thirty,

thirty-five or even forty years to pay off their mortgages. Concern that homebuyers were taking on too much debt, and that they'd be in debt for eons, caused the forty- and thirty-five-year options to be eliminated, which means your maximum is thirty years.

The thirty-year option is hugely popular for first-time buyers, and the reason is clear: lower payments. On a $250,000 mortgage at 5 per cent over twenty-five years, you'd pay accelerated biweekly payments of $727; over thirty years, the payments would fall to $667. The difference amounts to $1,560 per year.

I totally get the desire to keep payments low, especially when houses are as expensive as they're been in recent years. But if you can swing twenty-five years, do it. You'll save tens of thousands of dollars in interest along the way, and just as important, you'll have your house paid off in time to redirect money into registered education savings plans for your kids, as well as your own retirement funds.

MOVING IN

The list of closing costs earlier in this chapter will give you an idea of how much money you'll need to come up with to complete the purchase of your house. The meter does not stop running at that point, however. Far from it.

If at all possible, set several hundred dollars aside by moving day to cover the many incidental expenses you'll incur as a new homeowner. To start, there will be costs like pizza and beer for the friends and family members who help you move. Next, there are going to be multiple trips to Canadian Tire or Rona for odds and ends, and possibly more expensive excursions for furniture, lighting, rugs and such.

You'll quickly learn that the overriding financial rule for moving into a home is to do things gradually. But that said, be prepared for an initial cash outlay to get your new place in shape.

CHAPTER SEVEN SUMMARY

1. **Renting is okay.** Renting can be the shrewder move than buying if you cannot properly afford the full cost of buying and owning a home.
2. **Consider the relative benefits of RRSPs and TFSAs to save for a home.** You can pull money out of an RRSP using the Home Buyers' Plan, but you'll have to pay it back according to a schedule; TFSAs give you much more payback flexibility, and they let you keep your retire-ment savings tucked away for the future.
3. **Save intelligently.** Avoid trying for a big score in the stock market; use a high-interest savings account.
4. **Don't buy as much house as you can afford.** Lenders will allow you to buy more home than you can afford and still maintain your financial flexibility.
5. **Shop around for mortgage rates.** Establish what a good discounted rate is and then try to get it from your bank or a mortgage broker.

CASE STUDY: Nathan

Nathan, 32, works in sales, and his common-law spouse, Jen, is in marketing. After four and a half years of saving, the couple took a plunge into the housing market and bought a detached home in a community just outside Toronto. Let's see what we can learn from their experience as homebuyers and owners.

House cost: $540,000.

How much of a down payment did you have? Thirty-five per cent.

How did you save your down payment? We stayed in a rental unit for a long time, we until we had a significant down payment for our first house purchase. Also we had some money provided by parents.

Describe your mortgage: We currently have a thirty-year variable-rate mortgage in order to keep our payments low, just in case we find ourselves in a situation where there is a job loss. However, we do pay lump sums fairly frequently to pay down the mortgage as quickly as possible. We are pretty focused on paying down our mortgage debt currently because we don't have other responsibilities such as children or other debt.

Advice on arranging a mortgage? Make sure that you shop around and find the best arrangement for your own circumstance. Whether that be a variable- or fixed-rate mortgage, it really is a personal decision. Our belief is that the quicker you can rid yourself of a mortgage, the better off you are. We aren't fond of debt and think that everyone's situation is different, based on job security, pay, etc. It's called "personal" finance for a reason.

Where did you arrange your mortgage? We used a mortgage broker who was able to find a better rate than we could find elsewhere dealing with banks directly. By shopping around, we have been able to save a significant amount in interest payments.

What is your household income? Approximately $220,000.

What are your payments? Monthly payments of approximately $1,300. However, we are increasing payments significantly currently to pay off the principal amount. We took a longer amortization period just in case of job loss, but plan to pay off the mortgage much earlier than thirty years.

How would you describe the financial adjustment in going from renting to owning? The big difference we have found from renting to owning is the fact that we had to completely furnish our home. As renters, we knew we'd eventually move, which meant that we didn't worry too much about the decor. Our new home is significantly larger than our apartment, meaning there was a need to buy a lot of furniture. Also, there are costs we never had to worry about. Whereas we had all bills included when renting, now we have to consider the different costs for bills and other miscellaneous costs.

Biggest financial surprise as a new homeowner? We did a lot of research on the costs of buying a house, so we had a good idea of the closing costs. But it's the things you need once you move in that start to add up, even little things as small as a shovel, rake or lawn mower.

What was your biggest mistake as a homeowner or buyer? I would say that maybe we bought a house that is larger than required at this point. We could have bought a smaller home and then moved up in time, but we thought we should buy the house we needed out of the gate.

What was your smartest move in buying and owning a home? We have been very good at planning for different situations, and ensuring from a financial perspective that we were ready for unexpected costs and potential "bad" situations.

What was the biggest mental adjustment for you in buying a home? Owing money. Based on my upbringing, I've never enjoyed owing money, whether that be borrowing $5 for lunch or where we are now with a mortgage. Having that debt was really difficult for me, as I see it as taking away freedom.

What's your best advice for people who want to get into the housing market? My biggest recommendation would be that they plan both financially and emotionally. They should ensure that they understand the monthly costs, including all costs of home ownership, while maintaining the ability to save for retirement and for emergency situations. It's very easy to see what your friends are doing and get caught up in trying to keep up, but remember that you should stay within your means.

EIGHT

WEDDINGS AND KIDS

I'm no wedding planner. But I do notice a growing industry that caters to people getting married, and that worries me. Are people being influenced to spend beyond their means to make their special day a little more special? Weddings are one of life's most joyous occasions, so live it up. But just as you'll have to live within your means once you're married, so should you arrange a wedding that's within your budget.

If you're planning a wedding, you have complete control over how much you pay. Having kids is . . . well, different. Of all the life events described in this book, having kids will create the most profound, lasting and unpredictable impact on your financial situation. You may not notice. As the costs of raising kids take hold, opportunities for new parents to spend money on themselves will dwindle. They'll be paying for daycare, but they won't be travelling or eating at restaurants much. They'll be buying baby clothes, but they won't have time for adult clothes shopping. Having kids is such a happy event that it seems almost gross to talk about the costs. But let's do it anyway. Your baby won't mind, and if you can avoid a few financial pitfalls, you'll enjoy parenthood all the more.

WEDDINGS: YOU, YOUR PARENTS AND THE HIGH COST OF GETTING MARRIED

There is a tradition that the bride's parents pay for a wedding, while the groom's parents contribute by picking up the bill for something substantial like alcohol, flowers or the rehearsal dinner. Bottom line: society places a higher financial burden on the parents of girls than boys when it comes to weddings.

And what a burden it is. *Weddingbells* magazine—there's that wedding industry I was talking about—conducts annual surveys on the cost of getting married, and the most recent average total was $23,330, up from $20,129 in the previous year. This amount includes an average $5,287 spent on the honeymoon, so figure on roughly $18,000 as a ballpark estimate for the rest. Note that the biggest expense by far is the venue, at an average $9,500 or so. If your parents have a big backyard, I know a way you can save big money on a wedding . . .

Spending tens of thousands or more may be fine if your parents have been saving for years for your wedding, or if they can swing the cost of a big bash without too much trouble. But what if they can only pay for a big wedding celebration by taking on serious debt? Let's remember that weddings typically happen at the worst time possible for parents to be ramping up their borrowing. In their fifties or later, parents should be trying their hardest to get the house paid off and the line of credit paid down so they can focus on retirement saving. Added debt from a wedding just doesn't fit in with this theme.

One option to make weddings more financially manageable is for the bride and groom to pool their money with the bride's parents. You might want to bring the parents of the groom into this chat as well.

In Chapter Seven, I raised the idea of taking the wedding money your parents are offering and instead using it for a down payment on a house. The choice with the more far-reaching and positive financial impact is the down payment.

WHEN YOUR PARENTS SHOULD THINK TWICE ABOUT HELPING YOU FINANCIALLY FOR WEDDINGS OR ANYTHING ELSE

- When they have big existing debts of their own.
- When it means taking on new debt.
- When giving you money means having less for their retirement.
- When it reinforces the role of you, the dependent child.
- When you don't actually need the help.

MONEY TALK, PRE-MARRIAGE
Canadian men and women typically get married in their late

twenties or very early thirties, which means they'll ideally have had time to establish themselves in the workforce, pay down their student debts and start saving. Think of a wedding as one of the ways those early savings may be put to use.

Discuss the financing of your wedding with your parents first. As noted, it's customary for couples to get financial assistance from parents when they marry. But this tradition may be a vestige of days when couples married much younger and had no money of their own. A *Weddingbells* survey from a few years ago found that 46 per cent of couples pay for their weddings with their savings, while 32 per cent rely on help from family and 16 per cent take out loans. These numbers suggest couples who are engaged should be prepared to contribute some or all of the cost of their wedding, as required.

Planning a wedding can bring about a couple's first experience of financial conflict. Avoid it by making compromises between the two of you and then presenting a united front for all dealings with parents and others. That's your first job. Your second is to absorb the lesson that guides all smart money management: live within your means. In other words, be your own person and don't be influenced to spend money by pressure from family, friends or the clever marketing of people who make a living off the wedding industry.

Take jewellers, for example. Somehow, they've managed to foster the absurd idea that men should spend either two to three months' salary or 5 per cent of their annual pay on an engagement ring. Wrong. Men, buy the ring that best accomplishes the twin goals of fitting into your budget and making your fiancée happy.

Because they're a celebration with family and friends, weddings tend to invite ostentation. If you can afford to put on a big show, through either your own savings or those of your parents, great. If not, your options are to throw the best wedding party you can afford or go into debt to do something bigger. Just be warned that borrowing a whack of money to fund a wedding is a strikingly bad financial move.

What are your plans after you get married—travel, buy a house, have kids? Whatever you want to do, a big wedding debt is going to drastically limit your freedom to realize that goal. True, you'll remember a great wedding for the rest of your life. But you may also remember the extra financial stresses brought on by carrying a big wedding debt into your first years of marriage. The credit card people at Visa did a survey of married couples a few years ago and found that two-thirds of participants believed they overspent on their weddings. Men tended to say they spent too much on their honeymoon, while women thought they overspent on food, drinks and wedding cakes, followed by their wedding dresses. The people who participated in the survey said they got the best value for their spending on wedding photos and decorations.

TIPS FOR SAVING MONEY ON A WEDDING

- **Limit the guest list:** Invite only close friends and family. Consider online invitations using a service like Paperless Post (paperlesspost.com).

- **Be flexible on the venue:** The wedding is all about you, not the building where it all happens.
- **Limit the booze:** Two or three drinks per person instead of an open bar.
- **Avoid Saturdays:** That's the most popular, and thus most expensive, day to book many wedding venues.
- **Keep the honeymoon short and sweet:** Take a modest getaway after your wedding and plan a nicer trip on one of your upcoming anniversaries.

Use a talk about wedding finances to tackle the broader issue of how you and your spouse will handle debt as a couple. Suggestion: both you and your spouse should discuss your comfort levels with the idea of owing money on credit cards, lines of credit and mortgages. Do you bring debts to the marriage? Have you always had debt? Does debt make you uncomfortable, or are you oblivious? It's much better to come to a consensus on debt early on, as opposed to dealing with arguments that arise after the fact.

A quick rule for cases where one or both spouses are bringing debt to the marriage: devise a debt-paydown action plan, starting with the debt carrying the highest interest rate and then working down. Credit cards have the highest borrowing costs, so they almost always come first. Student loans could be next in many cases.

MONEY TALK FOR NEWLYWEDS OR THOSE WHO LIVE TOGETHER

The commingling of your day-to-day finances with those of a partner or spouse is a highly delicate business. On one hand, you're making a commitment to someone to live together as a couple. Shouldn't money be part of that? On the other hand, you may be coming to this partnership with a strong sense of financial independence that you don't want to give up. This feeling may be exacerbated if you've always been a pay-the-bills-on-time kind of person and you've married a pay-the-bills-whenever kind of person.

Let me suggest a compromise approach that will cover both sides of this argument: create a joint bank account for your daily needs and bill paying, while keeping your own separate accounts for personal needs. Here's a game plan for the joint account:

- Pick a bank—it could be a bank either you or your spouse is using already, or it could be a new bank that offers a particularly suitable account package.
- Sign up as joint account holders, each with client cards for ATM use.
- Get cheques with the names of both account holders on them.
- Arrange to have both paycheques electronically deposited.
- Set up online bill payments so your monthly utility bills can be paid from your joint account.
- Set up automatic savings and investment contributions.

To integrate the personal accounts you and your spouse have with your joint account, have a recurring electronic transfer set up so that each time both of you are paid, a sum of money is automatically diverted from your joint account into individual accounts for each of you. This is personal money not needed to pay bills or rent, and it shouldn't be part of your savings, either. The idea is to have a separate amount of money that can be used for personal things. Be conservative about the amount of money you transfer into your personal accounts—you want to be sure there's enough left in the joint account to cover all day-to-day spending needs.

It'll be most efficient if your personal savings accounts are at the same bank where your joint account is, but this is not essential. Money can easily be transferred electronically between banks, although it can take a couple of days for this to happen in some cases. If you're moving money between accounts at the same bank, transfers are treated as if they're instant.

Smooth operation of the joint account requires both spouses to discuss major purchases in advance to ensure they're feasible. By spending big bucks on your own, you run the risk of blowing the household budget for the month. Don't worry about a joint account cramping your spending style as an individual. As you acquire more financial responsibilities through your life—houses, cars, kids, retirement savings—you'll find you have less money for spontaneous purchases of expensive stuff.

Use the same joint/separate account approach with credit cards. Pick a credit card that suits you in terms of its annual fee and reward program, and then pick one spouse to be the primary account holder. The other spouse will get a supplementary card with his or her own name on it. Points earned on both cards will go into the same pot, which means you're doubling your earning power.

There are two reasons to have separate credit cards as well. One is to have a backup card in case your primary card is lost or declined. Another is to provide both spouses with a way of keeping up their own separate credit ratings.

FINANCIAL EQUALITY ISSUES AMONG THE NEWLY MARRIED

With a joint account, the underlying assumption is that you and your spouse are pooling resources to cover the costs of living your lives together. One way to reflect an inequity between the salaries of both spouses is to have the higher-income spouse channel more money into his or her personal account than the lower-income spouse.

Couples who keep separate accounts will have to develop a system where each spouse pays according to his or her means. A higher-income spouse might contribute two-thirds of the rent or mortgage, for example.

Now, what about day-to-day financial decision-making? My experience is that one spouse naturally takes on the duty of primary financial manager in a couple. Often, the other spouse is happy to hand over day-to-day financial responsibilities. Note to the primary financial person in a couple: Be sure to involve your spouse periodically, even if he or she seems uninterested. Resentments may build later on if the non-financial spouse suddenly feels like he or she is being kept out of the loop. Note to the junior financial person in a couple: The more passive you are, the more you invite the senior financial partner to act unilaterally.

BABY TALK

The emails I get from young adults suggest that couples are strategizing a lot these days about when they'll have kids. Unexpected pregnancies happen, and that's life. But waiting to have kids until you're emotionally and financially ready for them means you're acting like . . . well, an adult.

Whatever you imagine the cost of raising kids to be, and however ready you feel to bear that cost, the reality will surprise you. Start with the outlay for fixing up the baby's room; buying a crib, car seat and stroller; and stocking up on baby clothes. Then add diapers, baby food, toys, shoes and more clothes. Then add daycare, if both parents will be working, as well as fees for activities, the cost of a bigger car, summer camps, birthday parties, hockey equipment, tutors, piano lessons, driving lessons and, finally, college or university tuition. I'm going mostly from memory here, both because my boys are 14 and 17 as I write this and because parents love their kids and don't think of them as financial liabilities. And yet, that's what they are. So be prepared. Think about how you'll afford all the costs involved in having kids and the debts you may be incurring along the way. Some financial goals you'll want to have reached in advance of starting a family include:

- Pay off debts as much as possible, notably student loans.
- Move into a house and establish a financial comfort zone as a homeowner.
- Build savings for emergencies.
- Establish common cause with your spouse about short- and long-term financial goals.

MATERNITY AND PARENTAL BENEFITS: YOUR SALARY AS THE STAY-AT-HOME PARENT OF AN INFANT

The most important financial consideration in beginning a family will be covering expenses while you or your spouse is on maternity or parental leave. Up to fifty weeks of maternity and parental benefits are available to new parents, and the money provided will certainly help cover the loss of income from having a parent at home rather than at work. But many couples will still find themselves managing on far less money than they had when both were working.

Maternal and parental benefits are paid through the federal Employment Insurance program, which means you'll need to have been working and paying EI premiums to qualify. The amount of benefits you receive is calculated as 55 per cent of your average insured earnings, up to a yearly maximum insurable amount of $44,200 at the time this was written. The weekly maximum payment was $468, which is a taxable amount.

It's worth noting the broad details on applying for maternity and parental benefits because they determine how quickly money will start to flow. First, there's a two-week unpaid waiting period before benefits kick in (the government compares this to the deductible amount that you must pay when making a home or car insurance claim). Second, it takes about twenty-eight days for an application for maternity benefits to be processed. The bottom line here is that between the time you leave work and the time your benefit payments start arriving, there could be several weeks without income. Plan ahead.

Maternal and parental benefits are designed to provide mothers and fathers a fair degree of flexibility in taking time off with a new baby. Mothers are entitled to fifteen weeks of maternal benefits. Another thirty-five weeks of parental benefits are available to the mother or the father, or for both to share as needed.

Mothers-to-be, one last point is to check with your human-resources department at work to see if you're one of the fortunate few who is eligible for a top-up of your maternity benefits by your employer. Data from Statistics Canada shows that one in five mothers on maternity leave get top-up benefits, and the average amount contributed by their employers was $300 per week.

GET THE TIMING RIGHT

Mothers can begin collecting maternity benefits before their baby is born, or around the time they give birth. To get some advice from the federal government on the best time to start drawing benefits, call 1–800–206–7218 and press 0 to speak to a representative.

HOTLIST:
TOP FIVE FINANCIAL MISTAKES NEW PARENTS MAKE

1. **Overspending on baby items that will be of use for only a short period of time.** For every piece of equipment you're planning to buy for your baby, there's the basic option, the ultimate state-of-the-art trendy version and probably five other gradations in between. Which you choose is as much an emotional decision as a financial one. First off,

you'll want to buy the best, safest product for your baby. You'll also want the products that are most convenient, durable and usable. And let's be honest, you'll also be thinking hard about which products are fashionable, which are the highest quality and which might broadcast to everyone that you cheaped out.

It's your money and your decision, so you'll find no judgments here on what you buy. But I can tell you from my own observations as a parent that buying the best of everything will break you financially. Prioritize so that you have a few items where you'll spend big and others where you'll shop at Walmart, buy used or take a loaner from a friend or family member.

2. **Not thinking ahead about having the right vehicle.** News flash: placing an infant car seat into your vehicle and then fastening it properly is hard work enough when you have a four-door. If you've got a two-door car, you'll get tired of bending yourself into pretzel shapes after, oh, about the first week of your life as a parent. The reason for mentioning this is to get you to think ahead so that if you need to change vehicles to accommodate a baby, you can do it in advance and at a time of your choosing.

Whatever vehicle you end up with, think long term. It doesn't take many years for strollers and diaper bags to give way to hockey bags and sticks.

3. **Not spending money on just the two of you.** It's all about the baby at first, but eventually you and your spouse will be able

to get out for a few hours every now and again. Do it. Get your parents, friends or a sibling over to babysit and spend some money on dinner, a movie or whatever. Time away from home will re-energize you. If you can swing it without going into debt, try an overnight getaway once a year—just you and your spouse. It's even worth getting a hotel room downtown for a night or two.

4. **Not setting up an RESP right away.** As soon as you can, apply for a social insurance number for your newborn and then use it to set up a registered education savings plan. Toss in a little money whenever you can to take advantage of the matching federal grant money (more detail on RESPs can be found in Chapter One).

   You can set up an RESP at any time, and you can make up for missed contribution room in future years. But human nature being what is, you may find that a block of years have slipped by and you haven't got the RESP going. Remember, money contributed to an RESP compounds tax-free while left in the plan. Money you put in when your child is born will have seventeen to eighteen years or more to grow.

5. **Not having a cash reserve for unexpected costs.** You'll be spending lots of cash to prepare for your baby, but the chances are almost nil that you'll anticipate every need. So keep a few hundred dollars sitting safely in a high-interest savings account to pick up those few surprise essentials.

THE KID COST CALCULATOR

The U.S. Department of Agriculture has created an online calculator to help parents get an approximate idea of how much it's costing to raise their children. This is only a ballpark estimate, and an American one at that (healthcare costs are factored in). Still, it's worth checking out to put a rough dollar figure on the money spent on your kids. Web address: 65.216.150.170/default.aspx.

BACK TO WORK: OR, WELCOME TO DAYCARE

In families with two working parents, daycare will be one of the biggest fixed expenses after the mortgage. Statistics published on *Today's Parent* magazine's website (www.todaysparent.com/lifeasparent/childcare/article.jsp?content=20100302_173310_5996&page=1) have shown that the cost of infant daycare can range from $7,000 to roughly $14,000 annually across Canada, depending on the province, while in-home care can cost roughly $6,500 to $10,500. Costs decline as your infant becomes a toddler and a preschooler and then hits school age. Many families will find that daycare expenses are a factor until their kids are old enough to come home after school and stay by themselves until Dad or Mom comes home from work. In other words, get set to pay for daycare for well more than a decade.

TAX TIPS FOR PARENTS

Just as families have their own particular expenses, they also benefit from targeted tax breaks to help ease the load. Here's a summary of some key tax measures for families:

- **Canada Child Tax Benefit.** A monthly amount paid tax-free to families without high net worths and with children under the age of 18; use this calculator to see how much you qualify for: www.cra-arc.gc.ca/bnfts/clcltr/cctb_clcltr-eng.html.
- **Universal Child Care Benefit.** One hundred dollars per month is available for children under the age of six; this money is taxable in the hands of the lower-income spouse.
- **Children's Fitness Amount.** Claim $100 to $500 in costs for your kids' athletic activities and receive a non-refundable tax credit for up to $75.
- **Childcare expenses.** A tax deduction claimed by the lower-income spouse; the idea is to help parents pay daycare costs so they can work or go to school.
- **GST/HST credit.** A tax-free payment made quarterly to help people with low or modest incomes.

TAXING TERMS

Tax credit: Reduces the amount of tax you pay.

Tax deduction: Reduces your taxable income.

WHAT ABOUT THE GRANDPARENTS?

Your parents may want to help you with the expense of preparing for a baby, and these contributions can be a huge help. Cash is great, and so is a commitment to cover the cost of one particular item—say, a crib or stroller. After the baby is born, the best financial gift your parents can give both you and your newborn is a contribution to a registered education savings plan, or RESP.

I've been hammering away on the need for RESPs all through this book because I think they're essential in a world of spiralling educational costs. But as new parents, you may not have the spare cash to contribute to an RESP. Your parents can help out here. Just tell them to head to their bank or financial adviser with their grandchild's social insurance number. If they're unsure what to invest in, keep things simple by suggesting they consider a guaranteed investment certificate or a mutual fund that holds blue-chip dividend stocks.

In setting up an RESP, your parents should consider their age, health and the likelihood that they will be around for their grandchild to attend university. If your parents feel they might not be around that long, they may choose to make a lump-sum RESP contribution (the lifetime limit for a child is $50,000). However, for reasons connected to the federal grant money that RESP contributions attract, it can make sense to contribute on a steady annual basis.

Through the Canada Education Savings Grant, the federal government matches each dollar of contribution money with twenty cents to a maximum of $500 per year. This means that if you contribute a child's lifetime $50,000 contribution amount right after he or she is born, the child gets only $500 in grant money. Note that the lifetime limit for grant money per child is $7,200.

Despite losing out on the grant money, it can make sense for your parents to contribute a big lump-sum amount upfront when their grandchild is born. Having a big sum of money in the bank can be worth a lot compared to good intentions about making annual contributions in the years ahead.

One last thing for your parents to think about if they're making RESP contributions is to co-ordinate efforts with you. The $500 in available grant money per year and the $50,000 lifetime contribution limit apply to all a child's RESP accounts in aggregate, not to each individual account.

CHAPTER EIGHT SUMMARY

1. **Avoid going into debt to pay for a wedding.** Arrange the best wedding you can afford.
2. **Don't go nuts with the engagement ring.** Men, don't buy that crap about spending three months' salary—spend what you can afford and remember that you can always buy a nicer ring later on as an anniversary present.
3. **Prepare for the arrival of a baby by clearing the decks, financially.** Pay down debt as much as possible and build up savings to cover the miscellaneous unexpected costs of parenting.
4. **Mind the cost of daycare.** It's expensive, and in families with two working parents, it will be a part of life for many years.
5. **Grandparent alert on RESPs.** There's no better present you can give your new baby than a contribution to a registered education savings plan.

CASE STUDY: Meghan

Meghan, 29, is a Toronto teacher who is coming off an eventful year in which she both got married—to another teacher—and bought a house. Many financial lessons were learned in the process, and Meghan was generous in sharing them.

How long have you been married? Five months.

How did you pay for your wedding? The wedding cost $30,000 (honeymoon included), and it has all been paid off. I had inheritance money from my grandfather, and my mother helped us out as well. We were only a few thousand dollars in the red after all of the financial gifts were tallied.

Are you or your spouse paying off any student loans? Neither of us had student loans. I opened a student line of credit when I went away to Australia for teachers' college in 2006. When I came home and was no longer a student, it was changed to a regular line of credit. It is not paid off.

Describe the house you just bought: It's a detached, two-bedroom bungalow in Toronto.

What financial stresses do you have in your day-to-day life? Budgeting—being able to put away enough money in savings and for bills, after each paycheque, and still have enough to get by for the next two weeks. We have given up certain luxuries that we used to have when we were simply renting.

Are you planning a family? Yes.

Do you feel like you have a good sense of how much it costs to raise kids? Unfortunately, yes. The costs are most of what terrifies us.

What financial preparations have you made for having kids? We are trying to get our own budget in order first.

What's your biggest financial concern about having kids? The initial costs (crib, etc.) and, further down the line, paying for their activities and sports.

Do you and your spouse have a joint chequing account, or are you keeping separate accounts? We have a joint chequing account, as well as multiple joint e-savings accounts. We both have kept a separate chequing account, too. We also share a credit card and have a separate one.

Does one of you handle financial matters? Decisions are made jointly, but my husband makes sure all of our bills are in order.

Do you tend to agree on financial matters, or do you have some disagreements? When we were first married and had just moved into the new house, I would say that 95 per cent of our disagreements were about money. We have gotten better at listening to each other and have made lists of priorities that we try to stick to.

What do you disagree about? How to best spend the money we do or do not have (to use line of credit or just wait it out and save for something we want).

Financially speaking, how secure do you feel as a working adult and homeowner? We both make a fair wage and, in contrast to many others, don't have that much debt. However, we are both a little taken aback at how little money we actually have to work with each week. Thankfully, we are both in a profession where our jobs are secure and we shouldn't have to worry about losing our jobs or about wage cuts in the future. This is reassuring when we begin to panic.

What was your biggest financial mistake as an adult? My husband says he wishes he had never got a line of credit. I would say it would be that I have not started to put any money away in RRSPs.

What are your smartest financial moves? Paying off a great deal of money on my line of credit with each paycheque. We are also happy to not have needed student loans. We also bought a car, but were able to pay it off right away, no monthly payments with interest. We don't carry a large credit card debt.

What's the best financial advice you've received? Carry the least amount of debt possible. Don't carry a balance on your credit card if you can avoid it. If possible, put 10 per cent away from each paycheque.

Any advice you wished you'd received but didn't? There are a lot of costs we weren't prepared for when buying our home. It would have been helpful to have saved a little more first.

What advice do you have for young adults getting married and buying homes? Don't feel you need to do both in the same year. Be prepared to give up certain luxuries (going out, gym memberships, entertainment). Listen to each other and don't get insulted if you don't see eye to eye. You will need to give a little to get a little. Budget! Do your very best to stay within your budget (both for your house and for your wedding). Don't anticipate getting monetary gifts from most of your guests—family still loves a good gift registry. However, you can always return some things and use the gift cards to get something you need later. We were able to buy a good-quality vacuum cleaner with all of our gift cards. Did I mention BUDGET?!

NINE

INSURANCE AND WILLS

Insurance. Boring, right? I get that. Felt the same way until I realized insurance is an important financial tool you use to protect yourself against catastrophe. Your property—home and car—need to be covered, and when you have a family, life insurance becomes an issue. Sellers of insurance can help you size up how much coverage you need, but their prime job is to sell insurance policies. That's why we'll look here at the kinds of insurance young adults really need, and how to arrange coverage at a reasonable cost.

RENTERS INSURANCE, A.K.A. TENANTS INSURANCE

This should be your first experience with buying insurance. Anywhere there are students, there are cell phones, iPads, laptop computers and all kinds of other nifty electronics that thieves love to steal. That's where renters insurance comes in. As home insurance protects the homeowner, renters insurance covers the belongings of a renter against theft or damage and against liability arising from, say, a fire or flood that begins in a student's apartment or residence room.

TEN MOST COMMONLY STOLEN ITEMS ON U.S. COLLEGE CAMPUSES

1. Cell phones
2. iPods
3. Laptops
4. Cash
5. Bicycles
6. Books
7. Jewellery
8. Credit and debit cards
9. Materials used for identity theft
10. Televisions

(source: collegestudentsafety.com)

Renters insurance is not discretionary. Making sure you have it as a student going off to college or university is one of the first adult financial tasks of your life away from home. That said, your parents can help you out here, because there's a good chance it's provided, at least in a limited form, through their home insurance policy.

Ask your parents to call their home insurance company, agent or broker and explain that they have a child moving away from home to attend school. They should ask what coverage the home insurance policy offers for the son's or daughter's belongings while away. Some companies may place a dollar limit on the coverage, often $5,000; some may offer a percentage of the total coverage provided on the home policy, say 5 per cent; and some may not cover particularly valuable electronics or jewellery.

Next, tell your parents to ask about the all-important liability coverage. The cost of replacing some stolen items could be nasty, but it's generally doable. Liability claims due to fire or water damage caused by a student can be astronomical. So be sure to see if your family's home insurance policy extends liability coverage to you while you're living away, or if this coverage can be added at an additional cost. Expect this cost to be about $50 or so for a student living in residence.

Liability coverage for students sharing a house off campus may not be available through your parents' home policy. In that case, a separate renters insurance policy is a good way to go. Tenant insurance premiums range from $200 to $400 or so, with higher costs assigned to big cities.

RENTERS INSURANCE:
AN EXCERPT FROM ONE UNIVERSITY'S RESIDENCE AGREEMENT

"We will not be liable, directly or indirectly, for loss or theft of personal property, or for damage or destruction of such property by fire, water or other cause. We advise you to obtain personal insurance against such eventualities. We do not purchase such protection for personal property. Coverage can often be obtained through a 'rider' on your family's tenant or homeowner insurance policy, which should include liability coverage for injury or damage caused by you."

Deductibles—the amount you have to pay if you make a claim—are typically set at $500. Raise the deductible to $1,000 and you might save 10 per cent in premiums per year.

HOME AND AUTO INSURANCE

Home and auto coverage is essential, and that's non-negotiable. Banks and other mortgage lenders typically ask for proof of insurance, and you almost certainly won't be able to license your car without auto insurance. It's too bad, then, that the price of both of these mandatory kinds of insurance has been soaring in recent years. Double-digit premium increases year after year are not unusual, while at the same time insurers have been reducing the level of coverage.

The lesson here for people buying insurance is to be an aggressive comparison shopper. Use whatever tools you can—online comparison-quote websites, insurance brokers and direct-to-the-public sellers of insurance—to find the coverage you need at a reasonable cost.

SOME WEBSITES FOR COMPARING HOME AND CAR INSURANCE PREMIUMS

Insurance-Canada.ca	www.insurance-canada.ca
InsuranceHotline.com	www.insurancehotline.com
InsuranceRates.com	www.insurancerates.com
Kanetix	www.kanetix.ca

RESOURCES FOR LEARNING MORE ABOUT INSURANCE

Financial Consumer Agency of Canada	www.fcac-acfc.gc.ca/eng/publications/ insurance/uinsurance/uinsurance_toc-eng.asp
Insurance Bureau of Canada	www.ibc.ca/en/index.asp

HOME INSURANCE BASICS

Home insurance is particularly tricky to shop around for because there's little standardization in policies and coverage. If one insurer is much cheaper than another, you have to dig down to find out why. Pay close attention to:

- **Deductible.** Deductibles of $1,000 are becoming more popular than $500 ones because they can noticeably reduce your annual premiums.
- **Policy type.** Comprehensive policies cover your property for all risks (called perils), except those that are specifically excluded; basic or named-peril policies specifically list all the included risks for which you're covered; broad policies combine comprehensive coverage for your building and named-peril coverage for your belongings.
- **Replacement cost on personal property.** Your possessions should be replaced with similar items, with no depreciation for how old they are; watch out for coverage that provides the actual cash value, which is what used items are deemed to be worth at the time the claim is made.
- **Guaranteed replacement cost for your home.** Means that the cost of repairing or rebuilding your home will be covered even if it exceeds the assessed value of the dwelling. (Note: This is different from the market value of your home and the property on which it lies.)
- **Liability.** Covers injuries to others or damage to other properties; $2 million in coverage is becoming standard.
- **Additional living expenses.** Covers the cost of living away from your home while damage is fixed.

- **Sewer backup.** Essential coverage that may require extra cost.
- **Monthly or annual payment.** If you pay monthly, you will likely be charged a service fee of a few percent of your total premium.
- **Extra coverage.** Fine jewellery, deluxe electronics, antiques or unique home renovations may require special coverage at additional cost.
- **Discounts.** You may be able to save a small amount, possibly 5 per cent, by combining your home and auto insurance with the same company; having a monitored burglar and/or fire alarm will save you money, as well having smoke detectors installed.

CAR INSURANCE

Car insurance is government-run in some provinces, while in others it's offered by the private sector. Regardless of where you get your insurance, there are a few things to consider if you want to keep premiums as low as possible.

One is the type of vehicle you buy—four-door vehicles cost less to insure than two-doors, for example, while four-wheel-drive vehicles cost more than traditional vehicles with two-wheel drive. Before buying a particular make or model of vehicle, don't hesitate to get a quote from an insurance company. Deductibles have a big effect on your premiums—$1,000 on your collision coverage will save you a significant amount compared to $500. You can have the same deductibles for your comprehensive coverage (for damage not related to collisions). If you drive an old clunker, consider dropping the collision coverage altogether.

You may be able to further save on premiums by not driving your car to work and by keeping the number of kilometres you drive to a minimum. If you've bought a new car, ask whether it's possible to upgrade your coverage in the first two years so that you get replacement value rather than the depreciated cash value of the car in case of a serious accident. Another extra feature that is worth the money is accident forgiveness—that's where an at-fault accident is "forgiven" to the extent that your premiums will not rise as a result.

LIFE INSURANCE

The point of life insurance is to ensure the financial security of your dependents if you die. There's nothing more to it than that, although a good portion of the life insurance industry is devoted to making you think otherwise. Insurers have a variety of products that tout life insurance as a kind of investment/estate-planning tool. You may want to check this stuff out when you attain great wealth and have maxed out your RRSP, TFSA, RESP, etc. Until such time, your sole interest in life insurance is to protect those who depend on your income in case you die.

For this, you will need what's known as term life insurance, a blessedly simple product. First, decide how much coverage you need and for how long you'll need it. Then seek quotes from life insurance companies through online quote-comparison sites or by talking to insurance agents. That's all there is to it, other than a health questionnaire and quite possibly some sort of a paramedical exam where your height, weight and blood pressure are checked. Blood and urine tests may also be required.

The insurance industry sells lots of term life, but it's not very enthusiastic about it. Think of going to a nice restaurant and telling the waiter you'll just have salad. Expect to be told that term life insurance doesn't have any cash value, and that it will protect you for only a limited period of time, as its name suggests. All of this is true. If you don't die while your coverage is in effect, you've completely wasted the money you paid for it.

Well, so what? That's what insurance typically is: a product that's a waste of money if all goes well for you. Bear this in mind if you get the sales pitch for permanent insurance, which covers you until you die. Term life is much less lucrative for insurance sellers. Offered a choice between term and permanent life, the savvy twenty- or thirtysomething says something along the lines of "Thanks, I'll take term."

Term life is basically a commodity product, which means price is a huge factor in deciding which company you go with. The financial solidity of the company is important, too, although any reputable insurer will be a member of Assuris, the consumer protection plan for the life insurance industry in Canada. Assuris will backstop 85 per cent of the value of your coverage if your insurer becomes insolvent.

You may have some life insurance included as part of your compensation plan at work. While that's useful, you'll want to have some of your own coverage as well, in case you change jobs and end up somewhere without the same benefit. There are two key considerations in buying term life insurance, the first of which is how much coverage you want. When you arrange a mortgage with a bank, you will without fail be asked if you want to want life insurance coverage on your loan. Correct reply: "No thanks, I'll cover off my mortgage using term life insurance." Obviously, then, your first step in deciding how much term life coverage you need is to consider the outstanding balance on your mortgage.

Next, you'll want to consider any other debts that may be outstanding—say, a line of credit or a car loan. From there, you'll need to consider the needs of your family and any other dependants you might have. Specifically, there's the cost of your children's education (since you won't be around to make RESP contributions). Another consideration is your spouse's job situation. Is he or she working, and if so, is there enough coming in via annual salary to cover off the family's needs? (Remember, the mortgage won't be a factor.) If not, consider trying to replace your salary for a period of time. You'll also want to give your family a cash cushion to cover expenses such as your funeral.

There are online calculators that can help you work through the amount of life insurance coverage you need, and you can easily find some with a Google search. Prepare to be highballed on coverage, though. In fact, it would be surprising if you aren't told repeatedly that you need at least $1 million in coverage. If you can afford that, and truly believe your family won't be secure with anything less, then go ahead and book it. But most people will have to balance off coverage with affordability of premiums.

HOTLIST:

TOP REASONS NOT TO BUY MORTGAGE LIFE INSURANCE FROM YOUR BANK

- **Lack of flexibility.** Bank-sold mortgage life insurance pays— big surprise—your bank in case you die with an out- standing mortgage balance. With term life insurance, the money goes to whoever you choose. This beneficiary may choose to pay off the mortgage or not. Either way, it's his or her call.
- **Portability.** In short, bank-sold mortgage insurance has no portability. If you leave one bank for another when your mortgage comes up for renewal, you need to apply for coverage all over again. Term life lasts for however long a term you select.
- **Value.** The value of bank-sold mortgage insurance declines as the amount you owe falls, even though your premi- ums remain steady. With term life, your premiums buy you a level of coverage that remains constant throughout the term you've selected.
- **Cost.** Sellers of term life often claim to have cheaper premiums, but check this because much depends on your personal situation.
- **Sales tactics.** Banks can be pushy with mortgage insur- ance, and you may have to sign a document saying you decline the coverage; this approach tells you how much profit the banks must make off this insurance.

The second key point to consider in buying term life insurance is how long your coverage should be for. The kind of coverage you should be looking at commonly comes in terms of ten, twenty or thirty years, although fifteen- and twenty-five-year terms may be available as well. The ten-year term will be cheaper, but the twenty-year option is worth considering for a couple of reasons.

The first is that twenty years is a chunk of time over which your family will be most dependent on you and the income you generate. Let's say you follow the path of many parents and suddenly feel the need for life insurance when you take a trip with your spouse after the birth of your first child. You find yourself asking the question that lights up a smile on the faces of life insurance agents everywhere: "What will become of the children if something happens to one or both of us?"

Naturally, you decide to buy life insurance. With a twenty-year term life policy, you'll have your family covered through the entire period when your kids are young and at their most dependent. You may still need coverage at renewal time, but the amount will be much lower because your kids will soon be responsible for themselves financially. Also, your mortgage will be close to paid off.

A second reason to buy twenty-year term is that it can be a decent value. Competition between insurers has driven down ten- and twenty-year terms, which begs the question of why you shouldn't go with the cheaper ten-year option. The reason is that when you go to renew that policy after ten years, you'll be older. Your premiums will rise when you renew your policy, and it's possible they could rise to a point where it would have been cheaper to take the twenty-year policy to begin with.

And what about thirty-year term? It's going to be costly and may provide you with a longer period of coverage than you need. Saving money by going with twenty-year term seems a reasonable approach for people facing all the financial pressures of starting a family. Bottom line: always compare the ten- and twenty-year rates when shopping around for term insurance quotes.

HOW TERM LIFE QUOTES STACK UP

Here's a comparison of term life options for a 30-year-old woman who has never smoked and wants $250,000 in coverage. The quotes come from the insurance website Kanetix.ca and were accurate at the time this book was being written.

- **Ten-Year Term:** Quoted regular annual premium ranged from $145 to $167.50, but were as low as $115 for someone in top health.
- **Twenty-Year Term:** An annual premium range of $205 to $222.50, but as low as $147.50 for someone in top health.
- **Thirty-Year Term:** An annual premium range of $265 to $322.50, but as low as $217.50 for someone in top health.

WILLS

The need for life insurance is something that just about everybody figures out for themselves. Wills? Not so much. I've been surprised a few times over the years in hearing from parents who don't have them. Heck, my wife and I didn't have wills for a while after our boys were born. And then we remembered that we were adults with responsibilities.

The realization that you need a will often comes at the same time the life insurance revelation strikes you—when you're leaving the kids alone for the first time. Here's a suggestion: after your first child is born, find an estate lawyer and have a will drawn up. Okay, wills are kind of a morbid thing to think about just after you've had a child. But they're essential because they give you an opportunity to spell out exactly what should happen to your kids and your assets in case you die.

Notice how I suggested using a lawyer to draft a will. There are do-it-yourself will kits out there, and who knows, they might just do the trick for you at nominal cost. But drafting a will is one of those occasions where it's better to have something done properly than to have it done cheaply. So use an actual, live lawyer and forget the software. As for cost, expect to pay $300 to $500 or more, depending on how complex your situation is.

Your lawyer should guide you through all the questions that a will addresses, but basically these come down to who will be the guardian of your children if you and your spouse die, and how would you provide financially for their upbringing. Before going to the lawyer, think about which of your family members or friends you want your kids to live with, and then clear it with these people. Think as well about who you want to manage finances for your kids after you're gone.

It could be the guardian, or someone else. You should also choose an executor, which is a person who will manage the process of following through on your will. Remember to revisit your will if there are major changes in your life, such as divorce or separation, and when your kids have grown up and are no longer dependants.

While you're having your will drawn up, consider spending a little more to have a living will drafted. If you become sick or injured and can't speak for yourself, a living will would communicate your preferences in terms of care. For example, you might say you prefer not to be kept on life support if there is no hope you will recover.

CHAPTER NINE SUMMARY

1. **Students should absolutely have renters insurance.** It's not expensive and it can be invaluable if disaster strikes.

2. **Always shop around for home and car insurance.** Coverage may differ from company to company, but costs vary as well. Check at least three companies before making a commitment, and switch as necessary if you get a big premium increase on renewal.

3. **Buy term life insurance.** Young adults starting a family have a lot of expenses and term life is the most economical way to provide for a family in case of disaster.

CONCLUSION

I'm a personal-finance columnist not a sociologist, so I can't really verify my gut feeling that criticizing kids for being spoiled and soft is something parents have done for generations. You certainly hear a lot of grumbling about today's youth. They're lazy—too much time spent playing video games. They're disengaged because of time spent on the Internet and texting on their mobile devices. And perhaps most worryingly, they're spoiled by having too much given to them by their parents. There's a term that describes what some believe to be the root cause—affluenza, which means an affliction of the soul brought on by a sense of entitlement that isn't backed up by the drive to earn and achieve.

What doesn't get nearly as much attention is the range of challenges that young people face. Job markets are tight and the cost of the post-secondary schooling required to get ahead is rising sharply, with hardly a non-student voice raised in complaint. Housing prices in many cities are astronomically expensive, living costs are rising steadily and salary increases are often not keeping up. Plus, there are demographic changes what work against today's twenty- and thirtysomethings. An aging population means that people trying to enter the workforce are running smack into people who used to exit at age 65 but choose not to do so anymore for lifestyle and financial reasons.

It's tough out there, and young people need support to get off to a good financial start in life. Parents and grand-parents can help. Parents have no business running the financial affairs of their grown-up kids, but they can fill the role of trusted counsellors who have been through the exact same set of circumstances and learned a lot. This applies just as much to grandparents, who are often able to talk to their grandkids in a straight-up, I'm-just-here-to-help way that parents can't always manage. Also, seniors are some of the sharpest financial customers around. They have the experience, and they have the time to do their research.

Something that both the older and the younger generations may not yet have realized is how some of life's great financial milestones need to be reassessed in light of recent developments. We've lived for decades in a world where owning a house was considered standard adult behaviour. Today, as a result of the ups and downs of the housing market, some people should give serious consideration to renting for a while rather than rushing into the housing market. Car ownership is another example of today's change in thinking. Buying a car as soon as you were able to afford one used to be almost automatic. Today, with oil prices projected to keep rising, along with concerns about pollution and global warming, it's time to rethink the necessity of owning a car. Between public transportation and car-sharing services, some people just don't need their own wheels.

A broader financial theme is a growing emphasis on saving and investing and a de-emphasis—okay, a modest one—on borrowing. In a way, you could say we're edging toward a reconnection with the financial values of the years when Canadians were much more reluctant to spend beyond their means.

Don't read this as advocating a return to those simpler times, because that's neither possible nor desirable (people might have been careful borrowers in the past, but their over-all level of financial knowledge was lame). Rather, what we need to do is to combine some of the old financial virtues with today's much faster-paced world of information and personal empowerment.

That's what we've been talking about here in these pages— applying proven money-management strategies to the real world that people encounter as they enter college or university, graduate, move into the workforce and then start families. These are the years in which a lifetime of financial security is built, so they're vitally important. But then, you already knew that. That's why you read this book.

FIVE KEY LESSONS TO TAKE AWAY

- **Control your costs in university or college.** Borrow as necessary to afford a post-secondary education that will help you make a good living, then make repayment of your loans your top priority when you enter the workforce; treat credit card debt like it's radioactive during your student years.
- **Spending discipline now will pay off later.** Controlling debt and ramping up savings will give you much more control over when you reach financial milestones like buying a house.
- **Retirement planning starts the day you start working.** Set up an emergency fund first, then look at RRSPs and TFSAs as a retirement savings vehicle; put money away gradually to build a retirement fund while leaving yourself money for other financial goals.
- **Don't rush into buying big stuff like cars and houses.** Wait until you have saved a big down payment and can comfortably afford the costs of a loan or mortgage; renting isn't the financial gaffe it's sometimes made out to be if you approach it properly by investing the savings you realize over owning a home.
- **Prepare financially for raising a family.** Recognize the costs of having a child and factor this into your thinking about when to start a family.

AND NOW YOU'RE A PARENT: THREE ADDITIONAL LESSONS TO HELP RAISE FINANCIALLY SMART KIDS ·

- **Start teaching them about smart money management as soon as possible.** Start with an allowance when they're young and then mentor them as they start earning their own money so that they learn about the balance between saving and spending.

- **RESPs are your kids' best friend.** Massive student loans that take years to pay back are the only way for students to afford a full course of study in college or university unless they either take a few years off to work or have the benefit of RESPs set up by their parents.
- **Your experience is worth passing on.** Been there, done that. As they get older, your kids will be more receptive to hearing you say that about the financial questions they're facing.

INDEX

AcceleRate Financial, 73–74
accident forgiveness (auto insurance), 210
AccretiveAdvisor, 113
advertising, awareness about, 44–45
Advocis, 113
allowances, for children, 43
Ally (online bank), 73
American Express, gift cards, 50–51
amortization periods, 175–76
amortization schedules, 167
"anti-dowry," student debt as, 10
Assuris, 211
ATM cards
fees, 28, 66, 75–76
security, 77
auto insurance, 209–10
automated teller machines (ATMs), 28
AutoTrader.ca, 139

Bank of Canada, 33, 52, 172
Bank of Montreal (BMO), 72
Plus Plan, 67
Prepaid Travel MasterCard, 51
Bank of Nova Scotia (Scotiabank). *See also* Scotia iTrade
Momentum Visa, 88
Student Banking Advantage Plan, 68
bank statements, 76–77
banking
alternatives to cheques, 74–75
ATM fees, 28, 66, 75–76
chequing accounts, 64–65
children's accounts, 44, 45, 71
choosing a bank, 66–67, 72,

73–74, 90
choosing an account, 89–90
common mistakes, 75–79
errors by banks, 76–77
in-branch, 4, 66–67, 68,
   89–90
joint accounts, 187–89, 201
loyalty to one bank, 90
no-fee chequing accounts,
   69–71
ombudsmen, 78
online, 28, 44, 57, 76 (see
   also online banks)
overdraft protection, 70, 89
personal bank accounts,
   188–89, 190
phishing scams, 78–79
premium account packages,
   78
savings accounts, 73–74, 84,
   85, 118, 154, 157
service charges, 68–69
on shared computers,
   77–78
student accounts, 64–65,
   67–69
bicycles, as alternatives to cars,
   138
BigMama, 27
bill payments
and credit rating, 54
online, 57, 76
BMO. See Bank of Montreal
   (BMO)
bonds
exposure of RRSPs to, 108,
   109
maturing in July for RESP
   withdrawals, 15
owning directly vs. ETFs,
   106
as savings vehicle for a
   house, 157
BookMob, 27

Boomerang Generation, 2–3,
   90–98
bouncing cheques, 89
brokerage accounts, 106,
   112–13
budgeting, 82–87, 200–201,
   203
automatic transfers to online
   accounts, 85–86, 144
using websites, 86–87
while at college or university, 23–24

Campbell, Laurie, 54–55
Canada Child Tax Benefit, 197
Canada Deposit Insurance
   Corporation (CDIC), 73
Canada Education Savings
   Grants (CESGs), 11–12,
   14, 18–19, 198–99
Canada Mortgage and Housing
   Corporation, 164
Canada Pension Plan (CPP), 99,
   120
Canada Revenue Agency, 158
Canada Student Loans
   Program, 26
Canadian Alliance of Student
   Associations, 10, 11, 13
Canadian Federation of
   Students, 11
Canadian Imperial Bank of
   Commerce (CIBC), 70
CIBC Advantage for
   Students, 68
CIBC Aerogold Visa, 88
Canadian Mortgage Trends
   (blog), 166
Canlearn.ca, 37
Cannex.com, 170
Carpool.ca, 137
carpooling, 137
cars, 134–42
auto insurance, 209–10

bicycles as alternatives, 138
buying vs. leasing, 140–42
effect on credit rating of
    buying, 97
going without, 134–38, 142
graduate discounts, 140
and new parents, 194
new vs. used, 138–39
ownership costs, 135–36
car-sharing, 136–37, 142
case studies
    Jamie, 61–63
    Laura, 143–45
    Meghan, 200–203
    Nathan, 178–81
    Sarah, 96–98
    Stephen, 38–40
cash-back credit cards, 88
cheques
    alternatives to, 74–75
    bouncing, 89
chequing accounts, 64–65,
    72–73
    choosing, 89–90
    no-fee, 69–71
children, 191–99
    allowances, 43
    bank accounts for, 44, 45
    cost of raising, 196
    educating about finances,
        43–45, 145
    and financial mistakes made
        by parents, 193–95
    overspending on baby items,
        193–94
Children's Fitness Amount,
    197
chores, payment for, 44
CIBC. See Canadian Imperial
    Bank of Commerce
    (CIBC)
Citizens Bank of Canada, 69
Claymore 1–5 Year Laddered
    Government Bond Index

Fund (CLF), 112
Claymore Canadian
    Fundamental Index ETF
    (CRQ), 112
closing costs, 165–66
Coast Capital Savings Credit
    Union, 70
collision coverage, on old cars,
    209
company pensions, 120,
    126–32
    and changing jobs, 128–29
    group RRSPs, 127, 130–32
    tracking performance,
        131–32
    underfunding of, 132
compounding, 103–4
    and student debt, 30, 31
comprehensive insurance
    policies, 208
credit bureaus, 52–53
credit cards
    balances, and credit rating,
        54
    for day-to-day spending,
        87–88
    for emergencies, 49–52
    with high spending limits,
        40
    joint, 189–90
    low-interest, 56
    as means of building credit
        rating, 55–57
    misconceptions, 42–43
    no-fee, 56
    preloaded, 49–52
    reloadable prepaid, 51–52
    reward points, 88
    student, 45–49
credit counselling agencies, 55
credit lines. See lines of credit
credit ratings
    building, 52–57
    and buying a car, 97

credit unions, 66, 70, 73–74
Crosstown Civic Credit Union,
    73–74

daycare, 196
    tax deduction for, 197
Dayler, Zach, 24
debit cards, 28, 66, 75–76
    security, 77
debt, 41–60. *See also* credit
        cards; lines of credit;
        mortgages; student debt
    attitudes toward, 43, 52, 60
    and credit counselling
        agencies, 55
    and credit rating, 97
    discussing with spouse, 187
    to finance weddings, 186
    repayment as financial
        priority, 101–2
    RRSP withdrawals to repay,
        117
    and self-esteem, 43
    using to build credit rating,
        52–57
debt service ratios, 160–61
debt101.ca, 37
deductibles, 207, 208, 209
defined benefit pension plans,
        126–27, 129
    underfunding, 132
defined contribution pension
        plans, 127, 129–31
    management of, 129–31
    tracking performance,
        131–32
dividend funds, 111, 198
dividends
    definition, 111
    taxability of, 126
dollar-cost averaging, 115–16

education, 7–38
    budgeting, 23–24

cost, 7–8, 11
    deciding what to study, 23,
        25, 98
    financing, 11–20
    money-saving tips, 27–28
    planning for, 20–25, 195
    student debt, 8–11
    studying out of town, 21,
        25
    summer courses, 98
Education Assistance Payments
        (EAPs), 17
efollett (textbook rental
        directory), 27
emergency funds, 84, 168, 195
Employment Insurance (EI),
        192–93
engagement rings, 185–86
Equifax, 52–53
eRideShare.com, 137
estate planning
    life insurance, 210–15
    wills, 215–17
e-transfers, 49, 75
exchange-traded funds (ETFs),
        106, 112

family dynamics, 4
financial advisers, 105–6,
        110–11, 113–14
Financial Consumer Agency of
        Canada, 47–48, 87, 207
Financial Planning Standards
        Council, 113
financial priorities
    after graduation, 81–90
    budgeting, 82–87
    mistakes to avoid, 89–90
    of parents, 12–13
    and RESP management,
        14–15
    and retirement planning,
        101–3
First-Time Homebuyers' Tax

Credit (HBTC), 158
fixed-rate loans, 32–34
fixed-rate mortgages, 168,
  172–74
floating-rate loans, 32–34

gap years, 21–22
General Motors, 140
gift cards, non-reloadable,
  50–51
Golombek, Jamie, 35–37, 121,
  123–24
grace periods, 30, 31
graduate discounts, on cars, 140
grandparents
  contributions to RESPs, 13,
    197–99
  TFSAs for grandchildren,
    125
gross debt service (GDS) ratio,
  160–61
group RRSPs, 127, 130–32
GST/HST credits, 37, 197
Guaranteed Income
  Supplement, 120

Hamilton, Malcolm, 102–3
high-interest savings accounts,
  84, 85, 118, 154, 157
Holman, Mike, 19
Home Buyers' Plan, 117,
  154–57
home insurance, 163, 207–9
  types of policies, 208
home-equity lines of credit
  (HELOCs), 60
houses, 146–77
  closing costs, 165–66
  costs beyond mortgage
    payments, 161–64,
    176–77, 179–80
  deciding how much is
    affordable, 159–61, 180
  insurance, 163, 209–10

myths about, 147–49
pressure to buy, 154
price appreciation vs. stocks,
  153
prices, 149, 150, 158
readiness to buy, 164–66
renting vs. buying, 149–54
RRSP withdrawals to buy,
  117, 154–55
saving for, 154–57, 178
young people's perspective,
  5
hybrid mortgages, 167–68

income tax
  basic personal amount, 35
  credits, 36
  reasons to file return, 36–37
ING Direct
  Children's Savings Account,
    71
  interest rate on savings
    accounts, 73
  Thrive no-fee chequing
    account, 70, 71, 75
insurance, 204–15
  auto, 209–10
  deductibles, 207, 208, 209
  home, 163, 207–9
  liability coverage, 206, 208
  life, 210–15
  mortgage, 164–66
  renters, 204–7
  title, 166
  ways to reduce premiums,
    206–10
Insurance Bureau of Canada,
  207
Insurance-Canada.ca, 207
InsuranceHotline.com, 207
InsuranceRates.com, 207
Interac e-Transfers, 49, 75
interest
  on credit-card debt, 46–47, 48

on student debt, 29, 30–34, 36
taxation of, 157
interest rates
credit card, 48
and housing costs, 149–50
likelihood of increases, 174–75
on loans, 58–59
on mortgages, 167, 169, 171
prime rate, 172–73
relationship to bond yields, 109
on savings accounts, 73–74
setting of by banks, 172
investing. See stocks

Jamie (case study), 61–63
jewellers, 185–86
job markets, 94–95
joint bank accounts, 187–89, 201

Kanetix (website), 207
Kantrowitz, Mark, 23
Know Your Financial Advisor (website), 113

land-transfer tax, 165
Laura (case study), 143–45
leasing cars, 140–42
liability coverage, 208
for students, 206
life insurance
on mortgages, 212–13
permanent, 211
term, 210–12, 214–15
Lifelong Learning Plan, 117
lines of credit, 59–60, 144, 202
home-equity (HELOCs), 60
student, 26, 27
living wills, 217
loans, 58–60

co-signing, 55, 57
student (see student debt)
locked-in retirement accounts (LIRAs), 128–29
lump-sum prepayment, 168–69, 171–72, 178

Maclean's magazine, 94
maternal benefits, 192–93
Mazda, 140
MBNA Smart Cash Platinum Plus card, 88
McLister, Robert, 166–69, 171
Meghan (case study), 200–203
Mint.com, 86–87
mobile mortgage specialists, 168
Momentum Visa (Bank of Nova Scotia), 88
mortgage brokers. See mortgage planners
mortgage insurance, 164–66
mortgage planners, 170–71, 179
mortgages
accelerated payment, 175
amortization period, 175–76
"five Cs," 160
fixed- vs. variable-rate, 33, 172–74
fixed-rate, 168
grace periods, 31
hybrid, 167–68
life insurance on, 212–13
lump-sum prepayment, 168–69, 171–72, 178
pre-approval, 169
rate holds, 167, 169
shopping for interest rates, 167, 169–70, 171
term of, 167, 168
moving expenses, 36
mutual funds
definition, 106

sold by banks, 111
zero-load, 113–14

named-peril insurance policies,
208
Nathan (case study), 178–81
Nissan, 140
no-fee chequing accounts,
69–71
non-reloadable gift cards,
50–51
NSF (non-sufficient funds) fees,
89

Old Age Security, 120
Ombudsman for Banking
Services and Investments
(OBSI), 78
online banks, 66, 69–71, 73–74
automatic transfers to,
85–86, 144
online brokerages, 106, 112–13
overdraft protection, 70, 89

Paperless Post, 186
parental benefits, 192–93
parents
advice about RRSPs,
100–101, 105–6, 110–11
advice about searching for
jobs, 94
collapsing RESPs, 18–19
contributions to children's
TFSAs, 124–25
contributions to wedding
costs, 183–84, 185
co-signing of loans, 57
educating children about
finances, 43–45, 145
and emergency credit cards,
49–52
financial dependence on
children, 109–11
financial mistakes made by

new ones, 193–95
help with buying a car,
139–40
help with buying a house,
158–59
help with student debt
repayment, 35
importance of RESPs, 124
moving back in with, 90–98
new, 191–99
paying room and board to,
91–92, 93
and student credit cards,
48–49
taking time away from
home, 194–95
underutilization of RESPs,
12–13
Parsons, Laura, 4–5
PC Financial, 70–71
pension splitting, 126
pensions. See Canada Pension
Plan (CPP); company
pensions
permanent life insurance, 211
personal bank accounts,
188–89, 190
phishing, 78–79
PickUpPal, 137
Plus Plan (Bank of Montreal),
67
Post-Secondary Education (PSE)
payments, 16–17
President's Choice Financial.
See PC Financial
prime rate, 172–73
property taxes, 162, 163
public transit, tax credit, 36

rate holds, 167, 169
Ratehub.ca, 170
RateSupermarket.ca, 169–70
Rechtshaffen, Ted, 152–54
registered education savings

plans (RESPs), 11–19, 195
collapsing, 18–19
contribution limits, 13
contributions by grandparents, 13, 197–99
and eligibility for CESGs, 14
importance to parents, 124
investing strategy, 14–15
making withdrawals, 15–17
taxability of withdrawals,
12, 17
underutilization of, 12–13
registered retirement savings
plans (RRSPs), 100–127,
130–32
advice from parents,
100–101, 105–6
automatic savings plans,
114–16
compared with TFSAs,
118–24
and compounding, 103–4
contribution limits, 36
dollar-cost averaging, 115–16
early withdrawals, 116–18,
124
group, 127, 130–32
pressure to invest in, 97–98,
101–3
reinvesting tax refunds in,
121–22, 157
spousal, 125
starting, 111–14
tax refunds for contribu-
tions, 104–5
taxation of withdrawals,
104, 117–18, 122–23
transferring unused RESP
money to, 19
withdrawals to buy houses,
117, 154–55
renters insurance, 204–7
renting, vs. buying a home,
149–54

Repayment Assistance
Program, 34
replacement cost, 208
The RESP Book (Holman), 19
retirement planning, 99–133.
See also registered
retirement savings plans
(RRSPs)
by parents, 109–11
and sale of home, 148–49
ride sharing, 137
risk tolerance, 82, 107–9
Rosentreter, Kurt, 3
Royal Bank of Canada, 73

sales tax
GST/HST credits, 37, 197
on houses, 165
Sarah (case study), 96–98
saving. See also registered
education savings plans
(RESPs); registered
retirement savings plans
(RRSPs)
definition, 81
emergency funds, 84, 168,
195
for houses, 154–57
importance of, 80–81
for retirement, 99–133
savings accounts, 73–74
choosing, 89–90
high-interest, 84, 85, 118,
154, 157
scholarships, 20, 62
Schwartz, Jeff, 161
Scotia iTrade, 112
Scotiabank. See Bank of Nova
Scotia (Scotiabank)
self-esteem, and indebtedness,
43
Shiller, Robert, 152
Skype, 28
spousal RRSPs, 125

spouses
    discussing debt with, 187
    joint bank accounts,
        187–89, 201
    joint credit cards, 189–90
    personal bank accounts,
        188–89, 190
    responsibility for financial
        decision-making, 190,
        201–2
starting a family, 191–99
Stephen (case study), 38–40
stocks
    appreciation vs. housing
        prices, 153
    exposure of RESPs to,
        14–15
    exposure of RRSPs to,
        107–9
    fund primer, 106
    risk tolerance and, 81–82,
        107–9
    typical returns, 82, 108,
        153, 157
student debt, 9–11, 26–27
    calculators, 21
    credit cards, 45–49
    deductibility of interest, 36
    fixed- vs. floating-rate loans,
        32–34
    grace periods, 30, 31
    interest on, 29, 30–34, 36
    repaying, 28–35, 81–82, 101
Student Finance 101, 37
student lines of credit, 26, 27
Studentawards.com, 13, 20,
    23–24, 37
summer jobs, 20–21, 45,
    144–45

tax credits
    First-Time Homebuyers' Tax
        Credit, 158
    for parents, 196–97

    for student-loan interest, 34,
        36
    for tuition fees, 36
tax refunds
    misconceptions, 104, 123
    reinvestment in RRSPs,
        121–22, 157
    for RRSP contributions,
        104–5
taxation. See also income tax;
        land-transfer tax; property
        taxes; sales tax
    of dividends, 126
    educating children about, 44
    of employer contributions to
        group RRSPs, 127
    of interest earned, 157
    of investment gains on
        unused RESP money, 19
    of RESP withdrawals, 12,
        17
    of RRSP withdrawals, 104,
        117–18, 122–23, 155
    of TFSA withdrawals, 118,
        119
tax-free savings accounts
    (TFSAs)
    compared with RRSPs,
        118–24
    contribution limits, 118
    parental contributions,
        124–25
    popularity compared with
        RESPs, 12
    saving for a house, 154,
        156–57
TD Canada Trust, Value Plus
        Account, 68
tenants insurance, 204–7
term life insurance, 210–12,
        214–15
textbooks
    renting, 27
    tax credits for, 36

third-party aggregators, and
    budgeting, 86–87
Thrive no-fee chequing account
    (ING Direct), 70, 71, 75
Today's Parent magazine, 196
Toronto-Dominion Bank. *See*
    TD Canada Trust
total debt service (TDS) ratio,
    160–61
TransUnion, 52–53
TriDelta Financial, 152–54
tuition fees, 7–8, 11
    tax credits, 36

Universal Child Care Benefit,
    197
utility bills, 162

Value Plus Account (TD
    Canada Trust), 68

variable-rate loans, 32–34
variable-rate mortgages, 172–74
volunteering and networking,
    63

Weddingbells magazine, 183,
    185
weddings
    borrowing for, 186
    cost, 183, 200
    economizing, 186–87
    financing your own, 184–85
wills, 215–17
    living, 217

Zipcar, 136–37